BRITISH RAILWAYS ILLUSTRATED

SUMMER SPECIAL No.9

Welcome to British Railways Illustra

You'll Remember those Black and White Days...

LUSTRATED

Summer Special No.9

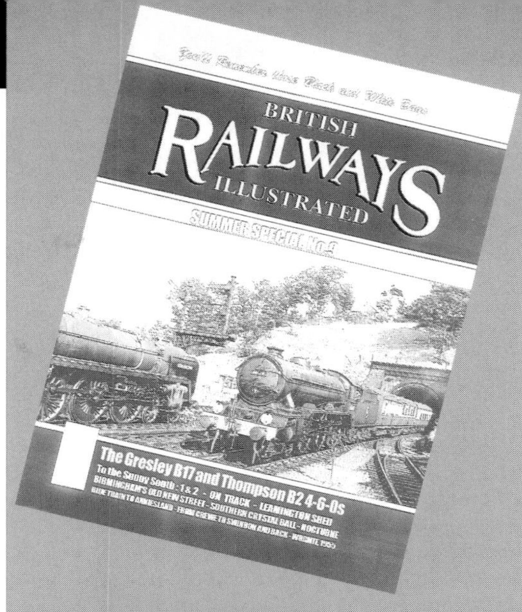

Cover photograph. Ipswich, some time in the early/mid 1950s. De-streamlined CITY OF LONDON has a down express running exclusively over GE metals, maybe only to Ipswich itself, for that is where the loco is shedded. The leading guard irons are retained, as is the original smokebox door. One of its successors, Britannia 70001 LORD HURCOMB awaits departure with (presumably) an express up to town. If ever a class of locos eclipsed so totally that which had come before, then it was the GE BR Class 7s. *See Tony Wright's account of the Gresley and Thompson B17/B2s in this Summer Special.* The Transport Treasury.

This page. 5077 FAIREY BATTLE ready to roll, in a classic George Heiron portrait.

Rear cover. The golden age of the British seaside holiday (the 'seaside holiday habit' as the social histories insist on calling it. Not many of us at the time realised it was a 'habit' – a 'habit' was something vaguely unpleasant). This glorious composition is the terminus at St Ives in Cornwall in the golden (we know they always were golden) August of 1953. The ten coaches of the Cornish Riviera Limited must have begun their journey on the line behind a pair of the small 2-6-2Ts. The leading one is presumably out of view to the left as the two engines disassociate themselves.

EDITORIAL MATTERS
Contributions, submissions, photographs or whatever (remember the contributor must address and attend to copyright), readers' letters, bouquets and brickbats for British Railways Illustrated must be addressed to Editor,

Chris Hawkins
at 59A, High Street, Clophill, Bedfordshire MK45 4BE
E-mail
Chris@irwellpressmags.demon.co.uk
Tel.01525 861888 or
Fax. 01525 861888 or

Printed & Bound by
The Amadeus Press, Huddersfield

IRWELL PRESS
No.1 in Railway Publishing

The Gresley B17

Notes by Tony Wright

Towards the end of last year I was commissioned to build 4mm scale B17 and B2 4-6-0s from different kit manufacturers, the results of which were published in journals catering for railway modellers. Part of the research into their construction was a 'phone call to our esteemed editor, begging for any spare pictures illustrating the classes, which would doubtless be scattered about the vast editorial desk. Quick as a flash, the pictures arrived, but there was a price; caption the pictures so that a visual history of the class(es) could be presented in the *Summer Special* for 2001.

While flattered to be asked/told, I must come clean and confess my relative lack of knowledge of these engines – well, first-hand knowledge at least. As the odd reader will realise I provide a lot of material for the model railway press, principally describing ECML big stuff, which is what I saw, day in and day out. The B17s and B2s were always relative strangers to me, for I only ever saw them at the extremities of their range, working the Harwich-Liverpool North Country Continental boat train. By the time I'd explored their more natural haunts, they'd all gone.

I won't presume to write a history of the classes, for this has already been done by those far more qualified than I – the RCTS 'Green Guide' complemented by *Yeadon's Register* Volume 5 remain, after all, the repository of more or less all that is known of these highly individual

d Thompson B2 4-6-0s

Above. **Class B17/1 2805 LINCOLNSHIRE REGIMENT at March shed on 25 July 1938, three months after its renaming from BURNHAM THORPE. I've been unable to discover why the name was changed from Nelson's birthplace to a regiment – perhaps a reader can enlighten us. Like 2800, 2805 is in original condition, carrying its GE style Westinghouse pump. This wonderful picture clearly illustrates the different painting approach applied to the short GE type tenders, namely the radiused corners to the green panel and vertical lining to the rear of the tank side – something not seen on other green-painted tenders. Photograph J.T. Rutherford, The Transport Treasury.**

Left. **Doyen of the class 2800 SANDRINGHAM at Stratford shed in June 1935. It's in more or less as-built condition, sporting the attractive LNER apple green paint scheme with the original NER type smokebox door. The top coping to the tender is clearly painted black, though some black and white photographs occasionally give the impression that this was green. From 1933 the class began to be subdivided according to altered springing arrangements, into Parts 1, 2 and 3, though how you would tell if 2800 is a B17/1, B17/2 or B17/3 purely from this picture is surely impossible. All these divisions were combined (sensibly) in 1937. Photograph The Transport Treasury.**

4-6-0s. What I've provided is but the briefest précis, but I have managed to expand a few points at least in the captions to these magnificent pictures.

Introduced from 1928 to meet the need for increased haulage capacity on the ex-GE main lines, the B17 three-cylinder, medium-powered 4-6-0s eventually numbered seventy-three examples, built over a period of nine years. Though officially a Gresley locomotive, it seems Doncaster had little to do with the final result, for it fell to the North British Locomotive Company of Glasgow to design and initially build a reasonably successful engine within the very strict design limits laid down.

Unusually for LNER three-cylinder locomotives up to that point, the drive was divided, with the middle cylinder driving the first axle and the two outside cylinders driving the centre. The Gresley derived motion was placed behind the cylinders, as in the D49s introduced the year before. This made it less prone to damage from smokebox ash during disposal. In appearance the original locos looked something of a hybrid. There was the classic GNR lazy 's' shape to the footplate at the base of the cab but they had NER type twelve-spoked bogie wheels, with an NER smokebox door too. Because of the tight length restrictions imposed by the GE 50ft turntables, a short GE type tender was fitted – to this commentator's eyes always a little incongruous.

Unlike the other members of the 'Big Four', the LNER never used 4-6-0s for its principal work, preferring Pacifics, Mikados or Prairies. Had the GE main line been up to RA9 standards, then such locos would have been built for that too. It was only the severe weight and length restrictions of the East Anglian lines that meant a 4-6-0 had to suffice.

Later batches were built to the same design at Darlington and by Robert Stephenson though those destined for the GC section were

As mentioned, the locos built for the GC section received Group Standard 4,200 gallon tenders and were classified B17/4. They were not originally Westinghouse fitted, though some were later, upon allocation to the GE section. Instead of country houses they took the names of famous football clubs on the LNER's home ground, instantly becoming 'Footballers' as opposed to 'Sandys'. 2851 DERBY COUNTY is on an up express at Nottingham Victoria. The date isn't specified but it's some time towards the late 'thirties. Unlike the first two pictures, and fully in Darlington's tradition, the cylinder covers are painted green. Either side of the football is Derby's colour, white. Photograph J.A. Whaley, The Transport Treasury.

given larger Group Standard tenders, there being no length restriction on the GC turntables. To many eyes, this produced a loco better balanced in appearance. Perhaps it says a lot for the LNER's attitude (and later BR's too) towards the GC where, despite it being 'RA9', only a moderately successful 4-6-0 was deemed sufficient to meet its needs. Certainly, there was some initial disappointment from the GC men, though, in characteristic fashion, they soon put in some stirring B17 performances, despite the fact that the locos quickly became rough riders. This propensity to turn rough, particularly near to shopping, afflicted the B17s throughout their lives, as it did most of the other LNER-designed classes lacking a pony truck at the rear.

I suppose it says a lot for the general satisfaction given by the class by how little, in the main, they were changed throughout thirty

A mystery photograph? This would appear to be an official works picture showing DARLINGTON at its birthplace, Darlington. However, the number 2849 means it should be bearing SHEFFIELD UNITED plates. DARLINGTON itself should be 2852. I can find no record of any official name changes and can only assume that this was a 'staged' picture – the real DARLINGTON still being under construction. One hopes the club colours are right, black and white instead of red and white stripes. Whatever, it's a superb picture, illustrating how well the ex-North Eastern works could out-shop a locomotive.

In September 1937 two of the class were streamlined in a mini A4 fashion to work the principal GE express of the period, the East Anglian. The train itself was not streamlined, nor did it run at streamliner speeds. The strange pair became B17/5 and were renamed; NORWICH CITY became EAST ANGLIAN and TOTTENHAM HOTSPUR became CITY OF LONDON. Such was the importance attached to the footballer names that both Canaries and Spurs subsequently ousted the country house names on two other locos. After the War both lost their streamlining. This classification illustrates how inconsistent the LNER system was, even though, at root, it's most logical. The B17s were subdivided (sensibly?) by virtue of different tenders and boilers (among other features) yet in other cases entirely different classes were identified by a mere subdivision – A2/1 and A2/2 for instance. On the other hand whole classes with numerous differences (the A4s, say) were not subdivided at all! 2859 was an object lesson in the perils of naming for the sake of local susceptibilities. Willie Yeadon (*Yeadon's Register Volume 5, Irwell Press 1993*) recalls coming across 2859 at Doncaster in September 1937, ready for a trial run and newly plated (on the smokebox side) with its old name NORWICH CITY. Confusion obviously then ensued for it then ran for just one day as the infinitely more dignified CITY OF NORWICH before becoming EAST ANGLIAN. A similar contretemps might well have developed for CITY OF LONDON, for both these engines show a hint in their paintwork of longer, earlier plates...

years of existence. From 1943 some were given B1 100A boilers, increasing their power. Thompson rebuilt ten from 1945 into two-cylinder B2s – a sort of bigger-wheeled B1, though none of these lasted as long as some of the originals.

As mentioned, when built, the class was responsible for some top link work on the GE and GC sections. Post-war, as more modern types were introduced, the B17s were relegated to lesser duties. The Britannias eclipsed them totally on the GE section and the arrival of A3s and V2s on the GC saw an end to first class work for them there, too. The North Country Continental remained a top job for them though, right up to the end of their lives. It is very regrettable that none survived to be preserved.

There's nothing on the back of this print to explain 2804's location and there's nothing to go on by way of background detail to even guess. So, what's to be said? ELVEDEN is in as-built condition, though it's beginning to need a good clean and is parked behind either another B17, a B12 or a D16 with green-painted short GE type tender. Again, the curved-corner style of outside lining is apparent on the tender, particularly clear on the one to the left. Note how the LNER on the tender is level with the numbers on the cabside on the B17s with GE tenders – it was placed lower on Group Standard tenders. There were subtle variations in the length of the nameplates fitted to this class – as a rule, the Footballers had ones extending almost the whole length of the top of the splasher, with the 'Sandys' being a bit shorter, irrespective of the number of words. Here, ELVEDEN has the extra length of nameplate left blank, unlike some of the A3s say, which merely spaced out the letters. As originally supplied, the first B17s from the NB had their names fixed onto the first splasher – like the Royal Scots, which were built by the same firm. ELVEDEN was the third B17 to be withdrawn, in August 1953, following LUMLEY CASTLE, taken out of stock the previous March and, even earlier, 61628 HAREWOOD HOUSE, in 1952. Strangely, this last one had become a B17/6, though why these three should have been such early victims is a puzzle, particularly as further withdrawals did not take place for a further five years. Photograph Gavin Whitelaw Collection.

Another picture with no location; like some locos in other shots, 2821 HATFIELD HOUSE is in original condition, and in full forward gear too – modellers please note. Though clearly a beautiful picture, it does betray a problem associated with older cameras, probably the sort fitted with the original double lenses. These rejoiced in the name of Rapid Rectilinear, RR for short, and could focus with crystal clarity in the centre of the image but fell-off at the periphery. The dodge was not to get too close to the subject. Photograph Gavin Whitelaw Collection.

The benighted Editor being an Arsenal supporter is the reason behind the inclusion of this picture. 'A typical nameplate, 28 May 1955' might be an appropriate caption... Actually, there was a peculiarity about the centre splasher which, while not apparent in any sort of 'face on' view, can be perceived in some of the other photographs in this collection. The centre splasher was very much wider than the other two, and was fashioned so in order to clear the reversing arm. Look out for this feature elsewhere in these pages. Photograph J. Robertson, The Transport Treasury.

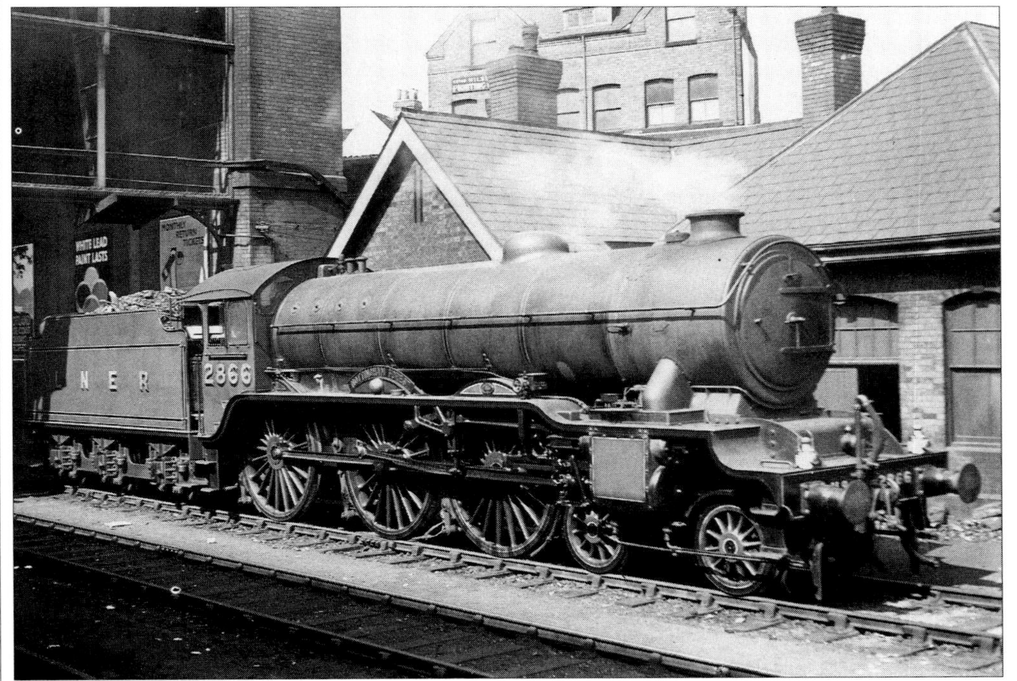

Left. Footballer 2866 NOTTINGHAM FOREST waits at Nottingham Victoria, to take over an express perhaps, or maybe it has just come off one (note reverse gear). It was new to the GC section in February 1937, so the picture could well have been taken in the summer of that year. As mentioned earlier, see how the company's initials are placed lower on these Group Standard tenders than on the GE sort. Judging by the green cylinder covers, Darlington has painted this loco though, curiously, the little footplate step just behind the steampipes is not lined out. Photograph J.A. Whaley, The Transport Treasury.

Class B17/1 2816 FALLODEN at Neasden shed pre-war, in company with ex-GC motive power. A small-tender B17 was slightly unusual on the GC, particularly when big tenders had been specifically provided for the route. It seems fair though – by 1939 all the locos with Group Standard tenders were cleared to run on the GE sections permitted to the short-tender engines. Unusually, the loco has had its cylinder drain cocks cut back. Photograph W. Hermiston, The Transport Treasury.

61619 WELBECK ABBEY leaves March with a delightfully antique stopper on 13 August 1954. This loco carries a B1 100A boiler and is classified B17/6, officially having been 'rebuilt' in January 1953. Rebuilding seems a curious description since the main visual difference is one more washout plug. The engine has lost its frame-mounted guard irons and steam heat pipe, though the latter was by no means uncommon in the summer when they were frequently removed for maintenance. Its tender, like all the class, is fitted for left-hand drive with the fireman's tools space on the right-hand side, though the division plate is much higher than standard. Photograph J. Robertson, The Transport Treasury.

THE ESSEX REGIMENT about to depart from Lincoln on 27 October 1951, perhaps on the Harwich-Liverpool North Country Continental. Fitted with a 100A boiler a year before, this B17/6 also sports a replacement smokebox door, more in the somewhat bulbous GN style than the NE original. It's also got the incorrect ('curly' instead of Gill Sans) style of six on its front numberplate. Originally named NEWCASTLE UNITED. The pipe runs from the lubricators in the cab to the coupled axleboxes differed substantially from loco to loco. Compare the shape of this one's on its boiler cladding to some of the others. Photograph R.H. Fullagar, The Transport Treasury.

The classic Liverpool Street shot, taken in September 1956, has 61647 HELMINGTON HALL waiting on the turntable. In reverse gear, the loco is in excellent external condition with the earlier style of BR tender emblem. This loco exchanged tenders with 2858 in June 1938, so becoming a B17/4 in the process However, this sub-classification was deleted in 1952 according to the RCTS 'Green Guide', so here 61647 is in fact a B17/1. Later, in 1958, it was to be reclassified B17/6. There's no doubt that locos fitted with the newer boiler were superior. Indeed, BR classed them as 5s rather than 4s when they were so equipped. Look how straight the lubricator pipes are on this loco. Photograph J.A.C. Kirke, The Transport Treasury.

Class B17/6 61642 KILVERSTONE HALL leaves March for Ely on 26 August 1958. Despite the express head code the train is described (quite rightly) as a local working, for it consists of no more than a Gresley CK, Thompson BTK and Gresley BG, by this time relegated to lesser workings as more Mark One stock was to be seen on the main line. A sister B17 waits on the adjoining platform road. Photograph Peter Groom.

RECOLLECTIONS

By Peter Coster

I remember them well, not because I saw large numbers of them at any one time, but because they were a daily sight on the GN main line. The Sandringhams in fact were among the first locomotives that I have any memories of. They were common north of London on the Cambridge turns into London. After the war the 'Sandys' were among the first to return to LNER apple green, and Cambridge MPD kept their engines on the Kings Cross turns in fine condition, very much a bright light in a predominantly monochrome world. I saw them at Hadley Wood, where I spent a great deal of time, graduating to Harringay in the south and Southgate, Barnet and farther afield as my years increased.

The B17s used were the original ones built for the GE Section, and I remember 61619 and her sisters were common sights. One could stand on the bridge at Greenwood plumb over the up main, and watch the engine rolling from side to side as she hurtled towards the bridge. Even at an early age I formed the impression that they were a bit lively at speed. Once I had talked to a few drivers I found that that was as understatement if anything, especially if they had one which was due for shops. Of course in those days the GE main line was less robust than it later became. Once I had a ride on one, and although working hard up to Potters Bar, the cab was swinging about as the engine strode uphill. It was not a hard, jarring ride typical of the B1, but an unpredictable side-to-side with a lot of bouncing. The B17s, as with most of Gresley's locomotives without a trailing axle, gave the rider the forcible impression that they had a tiger by the tail!

The B17 was initially designed by Kings Cross and Doncaster drawing offices, but the strict weight and length limits of the GE section defeated them both. The urgency of the GE Section's traffic problems was instrumental in the design being handed over to the North British Locomotive Company. Darlington drawing office advised, and the B17s emerged from Glasgow with a distinctly Darlingtonian look. The NB design broke one of Gresley's cherished principles in having divided drive, and allowed the use of the conjugated valve gear before the cylinders, so avoiding the need to allow for expansion in setting the valves. The B17s always had a far more even exhaust than their bigger sisters, even when run down. But otherwise, because of the strict limits of weight and size, some of the locomotive's heavier components such as the frames were less robust than they should have been.

One of the most obvious features of the GE engines was the short tender, necessitated by the 50ft turntable lengths on the GE. The later 'Footballers', Nos.61648-61672, had a Group Standard tender. Through the inescapable complexities of publicity etc, tenders got moved around; the rebuilding of ten engines into B2s was an opportunity to provide larger tenders, and spares of all sorts were used.

Cambridge had two B2s, Nos.61617 and 61671. The latter was the Royal Engine of course, and was always clean. I always thought that the reason for having 61617 as well as 61671 was that, with a short sighted monarch, the former might pass for the Royal Engine, although it had an ex-NE Atlantic tender. Even Royal Engines can fail at the last minute with an injector malfunction or some similar calamity. The other B2s were never seen, until the whole class came to Cambridge in the late 1950s. My main impression of them was that the weak frames of the B17s were not best served by conversion from three to two cylinder propulsion, with an increase in cylinder thrust of over 30% to be withstood. Certainly No.61671 spent long periods in Stratford Works under repair with cracked frames. With only ten engines, and unique ones at that, there were rarely any spare components to hand to speed up the process of repair.

The B17s were maintained at various Works. The LNER classes were allocated to all six LNER workshops for repair in addition to those pre-Group types already based there, and the B17s seem to have been passed round as capacity occurred here and there. Three Works were too far north. Stratford was the nearest to the engines' area of work but never seemed at its best in repairing more than two cylinders. Doncaster was the obvious place for a three cylinder express engine, but had insufficient capacity. It turned out that no Works repaired them for very long before another took over. There seems no particular reason for this gypsy existence, for they were no more difficult to repair than other classes beyond suffering with frame trouble.

Work

The B17s didn't seem to go down too well on the GE itself. Like its Works it was a two cylinder railway at heart and that is evident from the way in which the B1s were received and used in preference to the B17s. Witness also their attachment to their splendid 1500s. Of course the B1 was an excellent locomotive for the GE, and some of the best work of the class was done there. It was in truth a better answer than the B17, with its slightly smaller coupled wheels. Cambridge was an exception, and appeared happy running its B17s, especially on the GN main line where B1s were relatively unusual visitors.

Post-war, the arrival of large numbers of B1s tended to push the B17s aside. The arrival of the Britannias in 1951 pushed them further aside and although they still worked on the main line, they were seen much more on cross country duties which a decidedly smaller engine would cope with. It has to be admitted that 6ft 2ins or even 5ft 8ins was better than 6ft 8ins for stopping passenger services. The first engine, No.61628 HAREWOOD HOUSE, went for scrap in 1952 and after a pause a slow reduction in numbers accelerated with the coming of the diesels until they were gone. Unfortunately, although there was much good work, I know of no outstanding performance recorded on the GE to the B17s' credit.

On the GC Section matters were different. Here large numbers of the B17s were deployed, and some remarkable performances were noted. There was no doubt that the B17s could fly – presumably if the crew could hold on – and some high speeds were noted between the Chiltern ridge and Nottingham. One of the best was by Driver Tatlow of Leicester on No.2848, with 13 coaches, where the run was well up to Pacific standards. The GC B17s ran far better and travelled as far afield as Swindon and Newcastle via York.

Strangely, the B17s were hardly ever seen north of Hitchin and south of Doncaster, and after the war, not even north of Doncaster, unless going for repair at Darlington. The GC Section engines gradually migrated to the GE, and eventually all were in East Anglia. Cambridge turned to Nos.61652, 61653, 61657 and 61663, and these, with the Royal Engine, held sway for most of the time until the class was withdrawn and diesels took over.

The B17 boiler was a diagram 100, initially pressed at 200psi, but reduced to 180psi as a wartime economy. Later it was strengthened to work at 225psi instead of 180, and it became 100A. It was the LNER standard boiler for 4-6-0s and 2-8-0s, parallel with a round topped firebox, and it was an excellent, free-steaming and economical. The B2s were tested against the B17s, the engines being 61671 and 61627, a 180psi engine, and the B2 was the better. Against a 225psi B17, No.61622, matters were reversed, the B17 being the better engine. The performance of the B17s improved with the higher pressure as the 100A became the normal replacement for the original boilers. It served the B1 so well that I wonder whether the B17, with improved draughting, might have been a much better engine.

As I said earlier, they could fly. On the GN the most impressive performance I can recall was that of ROYAL SOVEREIGN itself. There was a semi-fast train from Kings Cross at 17.52, serving Cambridge and Peterborough, and to provide enough power to move the ten coaches up Holloway Bank, first a Pacific, and then a double heading was tried – I remember the A1/1, GREAT NORTHERN piloting No.61652 DARLINGTON one night. More typically a New England B1 led, drawing ahead at Hitchin to release the Cambridge B17 on the first half of the train. Then she took the rest of the train on to Peterborough. Since the preceding 17.39 to Letchworth with its L1 now became the problem in clearing the line to Potters Bar quickly, it was decided that the New England engine would pilot that train instead and wait at Hitchin, leaving the Cambridge B17 to earn its keep and take the ten coaches to Hitchin solo. Normally, from what I could see, the second engine during double heading contributed little more than black smoke, but with the one 4-6-0 a load of ten corridor coaches was a much tougher proposition.

No.61671 was a regular on the 17.52, and she went up Holloway Bank in style reminiscent of PENDENNIS CASTLE thirty years earlier, which Pacific drivers must have envied. The one thing that main line trains rarely did was to beat an N2 up the Bank, given an equal start. One could be at Finsbury Park long before the express came bustling along. On one occasion No.61671 beat the N2, if anything giving her a start. We passed the N2 and her quad-arts just by Holloway North, with No.61671 in full cry, her powerful bark deafening. If I remember correctly, we were standing in platform five in under six minutes. No wonder she broke her frames regularly!

The Cambridge engines were let loose on the GN track where familiarity and track quality obviously encouraged contempt for the speed limits, especially the 60mph limit between Kings Cross and Hatfield. I remember the ganger at Hornsey complained vigorously and often at the way the reverse curves were knocked out of line by up expresses travelling far faster than the 50mph allowed, and as a result a speed recorder was installed to test train speeds. The results confirmed the ganger's complaints, and the highest figure recorded was 85mph at around 16.30 or so. So the wheels of discipline ground round and the Top Link aristocracy in charge of the 'Elizabethan' was called to account. 'Not me' said an indignant driver, and the guard's log proved that he had been running early at 55-60mph. So back to the Train Register, and the culprit was discovered – a Cambridge man on a 'Beer' coming up in the wake of the Nonstop!

They were a handsome engine, and the design had the potential to achieve high standards. With a little careful development they could have formed a useful second string for the LNER, but that was not to be.

Below. **Class B17/1 RABY CASTLE ambles into Ipswich station on 10 August 1953, prominently displaying its headcode discs – though it has no train at this point. It still retains its frame-mounted guard irons and will never be upgraded to B17/6. Notes for engine pickers to make might include the rivets on the buffer beam and the wonderfully wobbly pipe runs from the lubricators. Surely the cab doors are dangerously out of gauge? Photograph J. Robertson, The Transport Treasury.**

At March on 5 August 1957, 61619 (compare with an earlier photo) now sports a new smokebox door, and a lower plate on its tender. It's on a through train from the Midlands to East Anglia, the loco having come on at Peterborough East. This illustrates the type of rather menial work performed by much of the class in the 1950s, hauling trains such as this, well within their capacity. The set appears to be made up of Stanier period Two/Three coaches, by this time relegated, like the loco, to secondary work. Photograph Peter Groom.

With less than a year left to it, 61627 ASKE HALL stands at March on 26 August 1958. Despite its approaching demise the March cleaners have nevertheless ensured she doesn't look too bad. By this late date the second BR emblem has been applied, though it's incorrectly facing the wrong way – something, naturally, never altered. Ironically, 61627 has reverted to the original style of smokebox door with its characteristic flange, smaller diameter and much larger radius of curvature in side profile. Photograph Peter Groom.

If ever a smokebox door altered the 'face' of a loco, this must be it. The GN style door has its hinge straps much closer together than normal, resulting in the numberplate being placed higher than was usual. Other than that HOLKHAM is a pretty standard B17/1, complete with Westinghouse pump. It was never fitted with a B1 boiler, though that hasn't prevented it from being diagrammed to take an up express. It waits in the centre road at Ipswich on 10 August 1953. Photograph J. Robertson, The Transport Treasury.

Cambridge shed plays host to 61608 GUNTON on 31 August 1959. The picture carries the rather cryptic 'note unusual feed to valve/cylinder' which is something of a mystery. More interestingly to me, as a railway modeller, is the state of the Westinghouse pump. These were renowned for their obstinacy, usually obviated by frequent bashes from a heavy tool, as clearly visible here. After neatly turning-up such an item on the lathe, how does one replicate this? Photograph Peter Groom.

61653 HUDDERSFIELD TOWN awaits departure from Kings Cross on 9 August 1954. It's double heading with a B1, not because of failure, but for diagramming purposes. This B17/6 will be heading for Cambridge, its home, on a combined train running complete as far as Hitchin. There the B1 will come off, shunt forwards and 61653 will take the front part of the train over Cambridge Junction, away from the main line through Royston to its destination. The B1 will set back and take its train to Abbot's Ripton or beyond. The B17s were regular visitors to the Cross, usually working out and returning on the Cambridge Buffet expresses. Photograph J. Robertson, The Transport Treasury.

Class B17/6 61654 SUNDERLAND heads a through express for the Midlands from East Anglia. It's leaving Peterborough East and is negotiating the junction to take it up to Peterborough North, where this loco will come off. The exquisite East elevated signal box is seen above the bridge, together with the very low bracket signals. Today, though the lines that the loco is traversing still remain (those going straight on have long gone) nothing is left of the station and the distinctive concrete bridge is used as a ground for the daubings of the graffiti brigade. Photograph Peter Groom.

The first to be rebuilt to B2, Cambridge's ROYAL SOVEREIGN runs past the station from the shed to take up the 3.15pm express to King's Cross on 26 August 1954. It will have already been up to town, to Liverpool Street and back during the morning. Originally named MANCHESTER CITY, the engine was renamed in 1946 a few months after its rebuilding to provide (almost) exclusive motive power for the Monarch's train up from Sandringham (the B2 coming on at King's Lynn) to Kings Cross, avoiding the formalities of the Queen entering the City at Liverpool Street. On this loco's withdrawal, in 1958, the name was transferred to 61632, finally disappearing altogether in February 1959. Photograph Peter Groom.

The end of the road for B2 CASTLE HEDINGHAM at Stratford in 1959. Awaiting disposal, the loco is nonetheless still in good external condition, carrying the second style of BR device. Its tender, like seven of its classmates, comes from an ex-NE Atlantic. The other three had Group Standard tenders (61671) or ex-P1 2-8-2 tenders (61615 and 61632). 61614's tender has had the coping filled in, though it still retains its curve at the rear. All you modellers who strive to get cab handrails perpendicular – don't worry too much! Photograph W. Hermiston, The Transport Treasury.

ARSENAL rests at Stratford, its home, on 19 December 1957. Nicely clean and glistening in the winter sunlight this B17/6 has been out of shops for just a couple of months and represents the final appearance of a Westinghouse-equipped Footballer. Photograph A.G. Ellis, The Transport Treasury.

A superb study of B2 61617 at Stratford on 16 March 1953. Points to note are the placing (typically for the GE) of the Route Availability numbers, beneath the lining in the middle of the cabside and the ex-NE tender, originally fitted to a Z Atlantic. This one still has the original ribbed coping to the top. The conduit on the rear of the tender was installed for communication between the footplate and the train, when the engine served on King George VI's funeral train in February 1952. Photograph A.G. Ellis, The Transport Treasury.

61617
FORD CASTLE

The rather cryptic note on the back of this print reads 'bad neg but interesting pic'. It certainly is, illustrating Liverpool Street in all its gloomy magnificence the early 1950s. The time is prior to October 1954, for 61643 CHAMPION LODGE became a B17/6 from that date and here, with only four washout plugs visible, she's still a B17/1. Both 4-6-0s, 61643 and the B1 61302 display ordinary lamps for their train descriptions – does this mean they are on trains to destinations beyond the GE system? Usually, as far as I know, GE trains carried discs rather than lamps, though we do have a case here of a commentator pontificating about things he doesn't know? Perhaps some locals can put this northerner right! Another observation – and nothing whatever to do with B17s – can a clever reader explain the siting of Broad Street's home signals (note the 0-6-2T) in the background? They face incoming trains to the terminus. Photograph The Transport Treasury.

March's own GAYTON HALL in the station at March on 12 August 1954. In excellent condition, as was typical for this shed's B17s, she appears to be waiting to take over an express. Details to note include an original style smokebox door (later in life she'll acquire the more bulbous sort) and prominent bufferbeam rivets – something not seen on all B17s. In the introduction, I mentioned my lack of widespread geographical sightings of the class, but this is one I remember well. Before they were displaced by Britannias on the North Country Continental (something greeted with joy by us trainspotters – what Philistines!) 61641 was one of the most frequently observed at Retford. Even more frequent was 61620 CLUMBER, and this pair seemed to monopolise the workings throughout the summer of 1958. However, the last time I saw GAYTON HALL, though on the same cross country road, she didn't have charge of the Boat Train. Pauperised, and not enough paper-round money available to cover the fare to Retford, days would be idled away at the nearest foot-reachable station to my grandparents' home, Kiveton Park on the section between Sheffield and Retford of the old MS&LR. The infrequent trains were mostly freights (the most exciting being 9F hauled), the odd B1-hauled 'express' to the coast, with the occasional D11 on a stopper. These veterans, moreover, had already been seen on the CLC line into Chester Northgate before their transfer much further east. Anyway, two trains aroused the most interest on this secondary line. One was the Pullman 'Master Cutler', recently introduced, though being diesel-hauled, any fascination it might have had quickly faded. The other was the 'Boat Train' though, as mentioned, only a few selected locos were diagrammed for this – until the ER Britannias appeared that is, though that is another story. To return to GAYTON HALL – on one blinding August day in 1959 (remember that summer?) the footbridge at Kiveton Park was our vantage point as an immense extra train surged through heading eastwards, double headed. 61641 was the train engine, piloted by J39 64741. My disintegrating 1957 Combined Volume records it, scribbled on the tattered end papers by the hand of your average, dimwit, twelve year old. Does anyone out there have a record of this working? Photograph J. Robertson, The Transport Treasury.

Underneath the coaling plant at Cambridge, home-based B2 61644 EARLHAM HALL has its tender replenished. With later style BR emblem on its ex-NER tender, this B2 is nearing the end of its days. Though in shadow, it's clear how the tender's coping has been filled-in and cut back into a vertical edge. Less clear in the dark, but just discernible, is the shallow support to the nameplate, unique to this loco. Fascinating as curiosities, the reasons behind the alterations and fitting of these odd detail differences between locos is now lost in time. Photograph The Transport Treasury.

With less than a year of life left, HUDDERSFIELD TOWN waits in the April 1959 sunshine at March, its home shed. Still fairly clean, they'll be no more visits to works where the incorrect right-facing lion can be replaced. An attempt seems to have been made at countersinking the rivets on her bufferbeam – Ah, the joys of loco-picking. Photograph Peter Groom.

In the empty country of the Glasgow & South Western main line through Dumfries, Michael Mensing sat one July day at the northern portal of Drumlanrig tunnel, north of Carronbridge. Top, Black Five 44820 approaches the tunnel with the 12 noon Glasgow St Enoch-Carlisle on 10 July and (below) sister locomotive (thought to be 44792) leaves in the opposite direction, heading north with a heavy train of steel scrap. Photographs Michael Mensing.

Above, on the same day, 10 July 1963, 45456 leaves the tunnel with a down freight. Below, seen from a rather more elevated viewpoint, yet another Black Five, 44785, heads south into the tunnel with an up train of mineral empties. Was there a better way to spend a summer's day? Photographs Michael Mensing.

To the Sunny South:1

'Bomo' Well, it is the Summer Special...

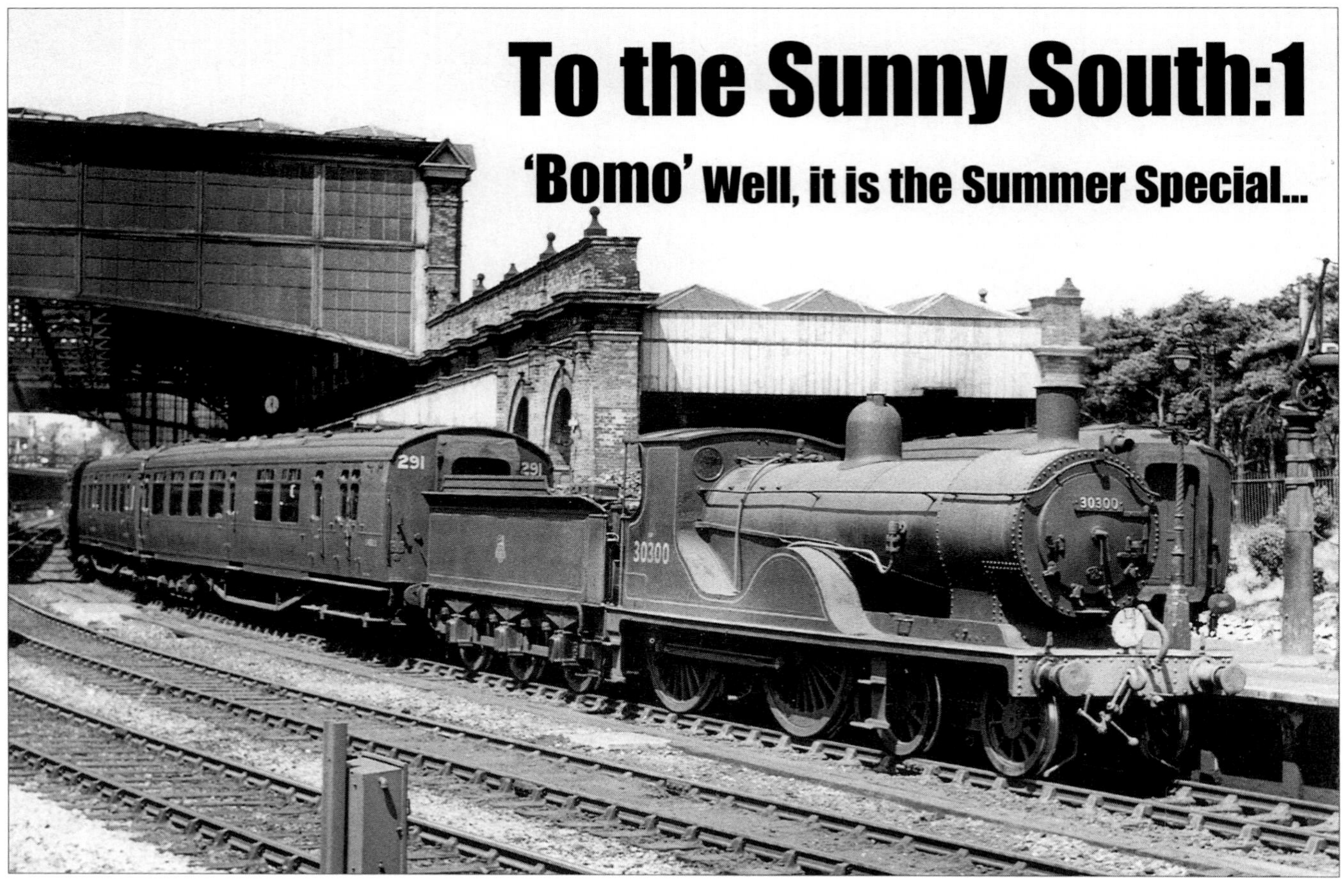

A 1950s summer at Bournemouth Central and Greyhound 4-4-0 30300 arrives at 'Bomo' (the old Southern code for the sedate seaside town) on a train from the west. The working is not clear, but the headcode applied to the Swanage branch. This was one of the T9s that had a wide cab and splashers and the six wheeled tender is a reminder that it once saw service on the Eastern Section. The barley sugar lamp post just beyond the front of the engine is worth a mention. Photograph T.R. Smith, The Transport Treasury.

Grimy 'Scotch Arthur' 30765 SIR GARETH heads an up express, Bournemouth-Newcastle, 25 June 1956. There was plenty of locomotive variety at Bournemouth Central on busy days. The overall roof added an air of dignity to this up-market resort, perfectly suited to the retired colonels of legend. Photograph T.R. Smith, The Transport Treasury.

Rebuilt Merchant Navy 35022 HOLLAND-AMERICA LINE on a Weymouth-Waterloo express, 18 June 1957. Coaches occupy the down through road; the track at the lower left-hand corner is the down platform road. Photograph T.R. Smith, The Transport Treasury.

West Country Pacific 34106 LYDFORD, on a Weymouth-Waterloo express awaits the right-away at Central. The Engine Roster carried on the buffer beam, 383, indicates the same working as 35022 above. Photograph T.R. Smith, The Transport Treasury. Thanks to Eric Youldon.

On Track

The Road Through Luton, 2 April 1950

Peter Coster

The southern approach, viewed from the up fast. The down and up slow are to the right, east of the fasts. Hayward Tyler Works on left. North of Luton in 1950 I believe that they became goods lines and as such would be worked under permissive block, with the proviso that absolute block could be introduced to permit passenger trains to be diverted over them.

The south end on the slows, shówing the extensive Crescent Road goods yard. There is an 8F coming up the slow in the distance. Beyond the slows is the middle siding for ECS exiting on to the down slow, then the fasts and the down siding beyond. There is a small ground frame. I cannot remember all of the signalboxes at Luton – certainly there was North Box and one south of the station by the water treatment plant. The run of the rodding suggests another further south, perhaps on the down side, but just what goes where is hard to see. The presence of an up slow distant on the post mid-picture also suggests another box nearby – it wouldn't be Chiltern Green's distant with a pull of two miles! I would expect the box to give release to the ground frame and to control the two dollies giving clearance from the sidings on to the up slow. It is a minimal ground frame and the yard points are hand operated.

The south end, looking south from the veranda of the signalbox on the down side south of the station, with the down fast platform a hundred yards or so behind the camera. The water treatment plant is immediately to the right of the wagons in the right foreground (note the lime spillage) which is prominent in the Bute Street and Clarence Road view. A train of coal empties double headed by 8Fs stands on the down slow, with the leading engine taking water while an express is signalled on the down fast. There is another water column on the down siding. I had many a tussle with that rotten connection in the foreground. It was right on the end of a transition curve leading off a curve of about 60 chains radius on to a straight through the platforms. The curve was limited to 70mph, later raised to 80 for diesel traction. Fortunately many services called at Luton, so were braking. It *always* rode badly and left its signature on the Hallade traces every time we took the whitewash coach over it. In the late 1960s we had twice yearly 'high speed' runs over the Midland and WCML often using D2 HELVELLYN which was specially maintained and authorised to run up to 100mph. I think 100mph was the fastest we allowed on the Midland, and the track was specially fettled in the known trouble spots. The trailing down fast connection at Luton beat us (me and the St. Albans PW Inspector) every time. We couldn't resite it due to the costs of signalling alterations, and the operators couldn't contemplate Luton without it. It was of course the only link to Dunstable in later years. The cattle dock is on the up side: it would be a strange sight now, as indeed it would be to find cattle anywhere near Luton!

This view is probably from an up fast bracket signal; it shows the GN branch from Hatfield, the GN sidings and Bute St. station in the distance on the left. It demonstrates how near and yet how far was the possibility of running straight ahead to Dunstable, then a village and now almost a city. The up fast has just been relaid, no doubt by hand. Crescent Road yard is on the right, with a resident 2F lurking inside.

The north end with an express in the down fast platform headed by – glory be – a Midland Compound. On the right is the parcels dock, and the goods shed is on the left. The single slip in the down fast was another cause of bad riding, but the layout had been simplified by the time diesels were running fast and reliably on the Midland lines. I am tempted to ask 'did they ever?' but that is a little unfair.

Mutual views of the north end and the bracket signals used by the photographer. The first looks north from Luton North box and the second looks south into the station. The bridge with its girders and the white hut are central in both views. What does strike the eye is the satisfyingly smooth alignment of the switches and crossings. The track is Bullhead and the gentle acceleration of steam traction had not knocked it about. One can understand how the senior engineers of those times (see *Britain's New Railway* over several issues of Volume 8) were reluctant to abandon bullhead in favour of flat bottom rail, experience of which was quite unpromising in the early 1950s. Solid stopblocks were permitted on non-passenger tracks, though I wouldn't like to depend on that earth-filled sleeper box stopping a 3F from dropping into the road below. What is interesting in these pictures is how unrelated the signals were to the criteria of the Railway Inspectorate and hence how signal sighting has been made so much easier in modern times. The R.I. insisted – rightly – that slow and fast lines signals should be in parallel i.e. side by side, so that a driver might not mistake a green on the down slow for the down fast and so on. Obviously the Railway Inspectorate could not insist that most of BR be resignalled to meet this requirement straightaway and so things stayed as they were until resignalling became necessary. Not only are the semaphores not in parallel but they are not in the driver's line of vision, 10ft above rail on the left side of the track. Some are high also, which improved sighting at a distance in clear weather but in fog they were a nuisance to the firemen who had to climb them to feel where the arm was!

LEAMINGTON

'A standard for all small capacity engine sheds throughout the system'

In September 1906, in the same year as Old Oak Common, Leamington shed opened. The giant Old Oak roundhouses had come into use earlier in the year and the two (very different) depots were both prototypes, if at opposite ends of the spectrum. Old Oak established the vast GWR roundhouse 'unit' depots (though none were ever built on this scale again) while Leamington represented Churchward's new type of small, comfortable, efficient and small country shed, a place at last pleasant to work in. So, it was in 1906 that the twin models of GWR shed developments were established – modern, well equipped and well laid out designs, built solidly and in quality materials (at long last, so far as GW engine sheds were concerned). Great Western engine sheds began to emerge from decades of tumbledown, gloomy neglect. Churchward's new sheds in that short spell from 1906 to the mid-1920s established the GW at the forefront of such provision, leaving behind for good the earlier grand efforts of the LNW and other giants.

Ian Sixsmith

All this has been said before in these 'engine shed' columns but it is a necessary introduction to the phenomenon of new building on the GWR in those years. The work spluttered to a conclusion in the 1920s and was not revived again

The classic GWR 'official' photographic portrait, which accompanied both *The Railway Gazette's* account and that of the *Great Western Magazine*. Not many pictures such as these survive, from any of the old companies which is a shame, for they have a striking, unreal look to them. These are the sheds (an astonishing one of Crewe South exists) the very moment, almost, before the engines and men were let in the yard and it is hard to avoid imagining them queuing up behind the photographer, anxious to get in their luxurious new surroundings, and out of the dump they had been forced to endure for some years past. The LNW lines run across behind the coaling stage. The concrete of the 'firepit' (as the GW termed the fire-dropping pit) and the 'apron' at the front of the shed would never look so bright again!

until Government money became available in the wake of the Great Depression. The new sheds were desperately needed to remedy the neglect of years; some of the original GW sheds were truly awful and Leamington was no exception. The shed replaced by the new structure in 1906 was a primitive wooden building dating from the early 1850s and sited to the west of the station. It was impossibly long – about 20ft wide but nearly 250ft long. There was only a single road, with turntable at the front and one spare siding, and it is safe to say that by its first half century of use, in 1902, the timber building would have been tired, to say the least. It had the decency to burn down in March that year, after which it was Hobson's Choice as engines stabled on the old shed road,

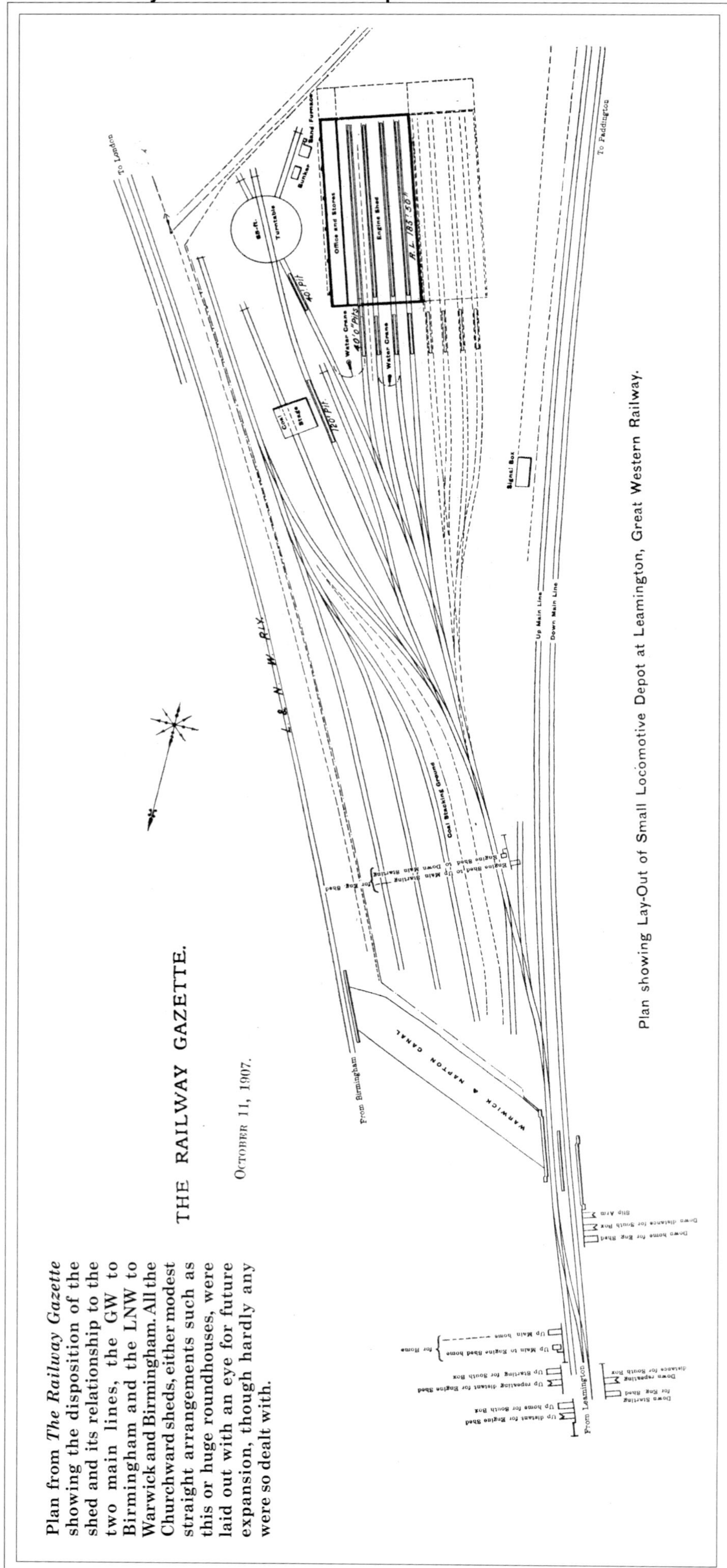

Plan from *The Railway Gazette* showing the disposition of the shed and its relationship to the two main lines, the GW to Birmingham and the LNW to Warwick and Birmingham. All the Churchward sheds, either modest straight arrangements such as this or huge roundhouses, were laid out with an eye for future expansion, though hardly any were so dealt with.

now merely an extended loco pit. With Churchward anxious to improve the pitiful stock of engine sheds on the line from about this time, poor denuded Leamington was an obvious first choice. As we have seen innumerable times before, these matters did not run quickly on any British line of the times and it was April 1905 before the Locomotive Committee confirmed that land for 'the new Engine shed at Leamington' was safely acquired and in the possession of the company. Shed, coal stage and turntable were estimated at £11,093.

The shed, along with Old Oak that year of 1906, caused something of a splash, and we are lucky that Churchward (no slouch when it came to showing off his products) invited the gentlemen of the press (in this case the redoubtable *Railway Gazette*) to inspect the new building. The shed came into use on 10 September 1906 though the new construction was not noted until the issue of 14 December, along with other items of interest that week; on the same page (it was still very much the railway age after all) were notes relating to the latest half-year earnings on the South India Railway, the latest six-months working results for the Great Indian Peninsula Railway, Russian flour and millstuffs rate increases, a landslide on the Midland requiring the diversion of London-Bradford expresses and many other points, including a full report of the seventeenth annual Great Northern Railway Athletic Association dinner, attended by Oliver Bury and H.G. Ivatt among others. The new shed was more completely described in *The Railway Gazette* a year later, on 11 October 1907:

LOCOMOTIVE RUNNING SHED AT LEAMINGTON, GREAT WESTERN RAILWAY

Towards the close of last year the Great Western Railway Company brought into use a new running shed at Leamington, of a type which it is intended to establish as standard for all small capacity engine sheds throughout the system.

The shed is situated at a point about half a mile to the south of the Leamington (Great Western) Station, on the up, or east side of the London and Birmingham main line. It is approached from off both up and down lines by a single road branching into several others, four of which run the whole length of the shed, while others serve the yard outside, which is equipped with a 65ft turntable, coal stage and other necessary appliances, to which reference will be made later.

The shed is 180ft long by 66ft wide and is built on the straight

Inside the shed; you can almost *smell* the paint. This is looking outwards to the shed yard – note the extra row of iron columns on the left-hand (west) wall, which would provide the necessary support should the shed ever be extended out over the railwaymen's allotments.

road principle, with pits extending practically the entire length of the four roads.

The roof, which is of the ordinary trussed type, is formed in two gables with an ample glazing area in each. The principals are of 30ft span and there are two rows of cast iron supporting columns, one between the two inner roads and the other close to the wall on the west side of the building. The presence of the row of columns so near to the wall is explained by the fact that on this side of the shed the company owns a large piece of land, at present occupied as allotments by the engine shed staff, which will, when occasion demands it, be utilised for extension purposes. It would then be an easy matter to remove the west wall without depriving the existing roof of its support on that side. Over each road inside the shed a smoke trough, communicating with a number of rectangular chimneys, has been provided, and hydrants are located along the space between the two inner pits for use in washing out boilers of engines standing on the adjacent road on each side. The outer roads are served by ground hydrants. On the east side of the

The shed in almost impossibly pristine condition. From the squalid open pit road to the west of the station which had served as 'shed' for some years, the new place must have seemed palatial indeed. Amongst the last of the work ordered in connection with the new establishment was laying 'a water main' (whether for locos or 'domestic' purposes is unknown) from the station, at an additional cost of £387.

The brand-new Leamington 65ft over girder turntable, built by Ransomes & Rapier of Ipswich. Some difficulty was experienced with it in 1916. It was described as 'badly in need of repair' and £150 was authorised to effect repairs.

shed there is a range of buildings comprising, in the order given and commencing at the northern end, the foreman's office, time and store keeper's office, lobby for men entering or leaving the shed, stores department, fitters' shop, containing bench with vices, smiths' hearth etc.; engine-men's mess room, with hot and cold water, cooking range, etc; a cleaners mess room and, finally, lavatories.

Outside in the yard is a sand drying and lighting up furnace with a capacity sufficient for supplying 15 engines. Near this is the 65ft turntable of the over girder type, while a little further away is the coaling stage, measuring 32ft by 30ft and provided with a single tip. A water tank, having a capacity of 45,000 gallons, is built on the top of the coal stage. Each of the four roads leading into the shed has a pit 40ft in length just outside the building, and a pit of the same length is provided in the approach to the turntable. Finally, a pit, 120ft

For facility of reference, the buildings are summarised below :—

Building.	Dimensions.
Engine Shed	180' × 66'.
Span of Principals	30'.
Height of Shoe	18'.
Walls	1' 1¼".
Stores	50' × 14'.
Fitting Shop	33' × 14'.
Engineers' and Cleaners' Messroom	40' × 14'.
Offices, etc.	32' × 14'.
Lavatories	11' × 14'.
Coal Stage	30' × 32'.
Tank—capacity	45,000 gallons.
Sand Furnace	12' × 10'.
Bunker	14' × 7'.
Total area of buildings (approx.)	15,500 sq. ft.

The old engine shed, a wooden structure, 237 feet by 20 feet by 23 feet, was totally destroyed by fire in March, 1902.

Note from a piece in the *Great Western Magazine* late in 1906, specifying the various dimensions.

Leamington in the murk, with one of the 0-6-2Ts which later disappeared from the complement (only to return before the end) outside the shed. The *Railway Gazette* plan reveals that when first laid out the land on the west side was simply left for when it might be needed. It wasn't, at least for shed purposes, but did prove a handy site for an engine release line and carriage sidings – partly visible at the right of this photograph. These were later put to use for the DMUs which took over many services from the 2-6-2Ts in the late 1950s.

The shed in late GW days, with 2-6-2T 8100 (which seems to have been something of a long-term resident) prominent.

long, is situated alongside the coal stage. The shed, which will accommodate 12 locomotives with tenders, or 15 engines of assorted types, is lighted by incandescent gas.

We are indebted to Mr G.J. Churchward, M.Inst.C.E. for permission to view the shed, and also to his divisional locomotive and carriage superintendent at Wolverhampton, Mr James A. Robinson M.Inst.M.E. who kindly met our representative at Leamington and explained matters on the spot.

The old shed had had an allocation of a dozen or so engines at the time it burned down – mainly 0-6-0s and 0-4-2Ts but this rose steadily over the years. By early BR days there were over thirty, including a Hall, a Grange, a Manor and a even a Saint. By then most of the complement was made up of a dozen 2-6-2Ts, mainly in the 51XX series. Later a pair of diesel cars was allocated, for Stratford services.

Work in the early 1950s was mainly concerned with local passenger services (hence the 2-6-2Ts – which also did banking at Hatton) from Leamington to Birmingham and Stratford, with only the odd job beyond. For more exacting work over longer distances there were the four disparate 4-6-0s. For freight a WD 2-8-0, three 2-8-2Ts and five 0-6-2Ts sufficed, along with four pannier tanks for the local yards and trips. 1952 saw a drop in the complement to just twenty-two steam locos, mainly due to loss of work on the introduction of through freights between Nuneaton and Banbury via Leamington. This saw off the 72XX 2-8-2Ts (which had worked some of the Leamington-Banbury trips) and most of the 4-6-0s, leaving just the Saint clinging on (just). Withdrawn in 1946, double framed 0-6-0T 1287 was still in place as a stationary boiler for washing out well into 1950 and lasted in fact until March 1953. It then finally succumbed to cracked tubes and was despatched to Swindon for scrap, with Croes Newydd's 0-4-2T 5811 as temporary replacement.

Under the Shed Foreman and the Running Foreman were two clerks and some seventy crews for thirty-odd engines, twenty more on 'shed grades' a dozen fitters, assistants and other mechanics, and two boilersmiths and an assistant.

The WDs remained the only tender locos at the shed until 4933 HIMLEY HALL arrived in January 1958, for a seven month stay. A BR Standard 2-6-2T had a short stay in June the same year. In September 1963 Leamington surrendered to the inevitable, passing to the London Midland Region on absorption of much of the old GW territory south and west of Birmingham. It became 2L in this foreign scheme of things but it was October 1964 before a mass clear out of all things GWR took place and the last five 2-6-2Ts were replaced on local goods and trip work by Ivatt 2-6-0s, 46428, 46442, 46457, 46470 and 46505. At the same time BR Standard Class 5s 73026, 73066, 73069 and 73156 arrived for the stone and cement trains from Harbury. They joined another Standard already there, 2-6-4T 80072 which had been at Leamington since September 1963. At about the same time banking ceased at Stratford on Avon releasing Leamington's three 2251 0-6-0s, two for scrap and one for Banbury. All this left the shed with just three ex-GW 0-6-2Ts at closure on 14 June 1965 – 6644, 6671 and 6697, along with the Ivatts and the Standards. The stationary boiler still remained at closure, in the shape of pannier tank 7734, withdrawn from Old Oak as far back as March 1959.

After closure railcars still used the premises in between passenger and parcels workings, with Nuneaton providing for the remaining loco hauled thrice-daily Leamington-Nuneaton parcels. Tyseley supplied 350hp diesel shunters, changed every two weeks, to cover the old LMS and GW yards.

Leamington shed in the 1930s. The windows at the rear wall show that the building could easily be extended out the back, too.

2-6-2T 5134 (renumbered from the 31XX series) alongside the coal stage; coupled to the loco coal wagon it presumably is, or has been, working as the yard pilot. The 45,000 gallon water tank was supplied under gravity from a reservoir at Budbrook.

4112, a much later 2-6-2T (some thirty years younger than 5134 for instance), on the 'firepit' in 1958. By this time Leamington was using about 300 tons of coal and generating three or four wagonloads of ash a week, somewhat down from a peak in earlier BR days. The coaler had originally had a single tip on the yard side (see the picture of 5134 for instance) but later on two were provided, as plainly shown here. One gave a tipping height of 11ft. 8in. but one was later fitted with an electrical hoist to give a better tipping height, of 14ft..

Leamington on 25 April 1954. Engines came into the yard on the single access road, which served for incoming as well as outgoing locos. Those coming on shed proceeded straight to the coaling road, first for ash cleaning then for coaling, before moving onto the turntable and then back again to the yard. Photograph W. Potter.

The shed on 15 May 1960; the view shows how the carriage sidings were converted for DMUs, with electric lighting and so on. LM locos seem to have been regular visitors from late 1958 onwards. By the time of closure in 1965, with something like two years of LM 'ownership' the complement would presumably have gone much the way of Banbury, Tyseley and so on, converting extensively to Black 5s, 8Fs, 9Fs and so on. Photograph Ken Fairey.

Ex-GW, LM types and diesels late in the day, 9 August 1964. Photograph W. Potter.

BIRMINGHAM'S

For anyone too young actually to remember when The Beatles first featured in the pop charts, the words 'Birmingham New Street' probably suggest a concrete slab shopping centre with Underground-like platforms beneath. However, even such youthful readers may well have some idea of what was there before 1966, from photographs published over the years. If, like me, you're (very much) the wrong side of 45 and have any interest in Britain's railways, you probably retain vivid memories of the old New Street. For either age group I hope to conjure up a coherent sketch of the station as I remember it in the 1950s and 1960s.

My photographs date back no earlier than 1955/56, but the structure had changed very little for decades, apart from the regrettable removal of the overall roof on the LNW side. I have vague memories of having seen the roof a handful of times as a boy, before it was dismantled in 1947. The attentions of the Luftwaffe in 1941/42 certainly hastened its demise but it had survived for 93 years – longer than did the twin roofs on the Midland side, as it turned out. The utilitarian replacement canopies were not visually appealing!

In the 1830s the London & Birmingham Railway was of course pivotal in the development of the new form of transport and it was this company which initiated the construction of a central station in Birmingham, completed in 1854. By

Notes and Photographs by
Michael Mensing

that time, the original stations on the east side of the city at Curzon Street (one each for the L&B and Grand Junction Railways) and Lawley Street (Birmingham & Derby Junction Railway) had become hopelessly inconvenient. This grand new station project brought great benefits to the booming industrial centre. Amalgamations of the London & Birmingham and Grand Junction into the LNWR and of the Birmingham & Derby Junction and Birmingham & Gloucester into the Midland Railway, meant now that Birmingham had a simpler, more unified passenger centre. At that time, however, only the north (LNW) side of the station existed, the Midland trains having no outlet to the south-west. They continued to use the original B&G route avoiding the city, running only local connections into and out of New Street from Camp Hill and Saltley.

The spectacular growth of Birmingham, along with other industrial centres in the latter half of the 19th century, obliged the Midland soon to undertake the task of creating its own route into New Street from King's Norton on the south-west outskirts. The existing Birmingham West Suburban Railway was largely utilised for this purpose. The Midland also built its own station on the south side of the layout, thus in 1885 establishing the basic structures and pattern of operations which were to survive until the 1960s rebuilding. I think that bit of historical background puts the old New Street into perspective: the rest is mainly reminiscences!

***

LD NEW STREET

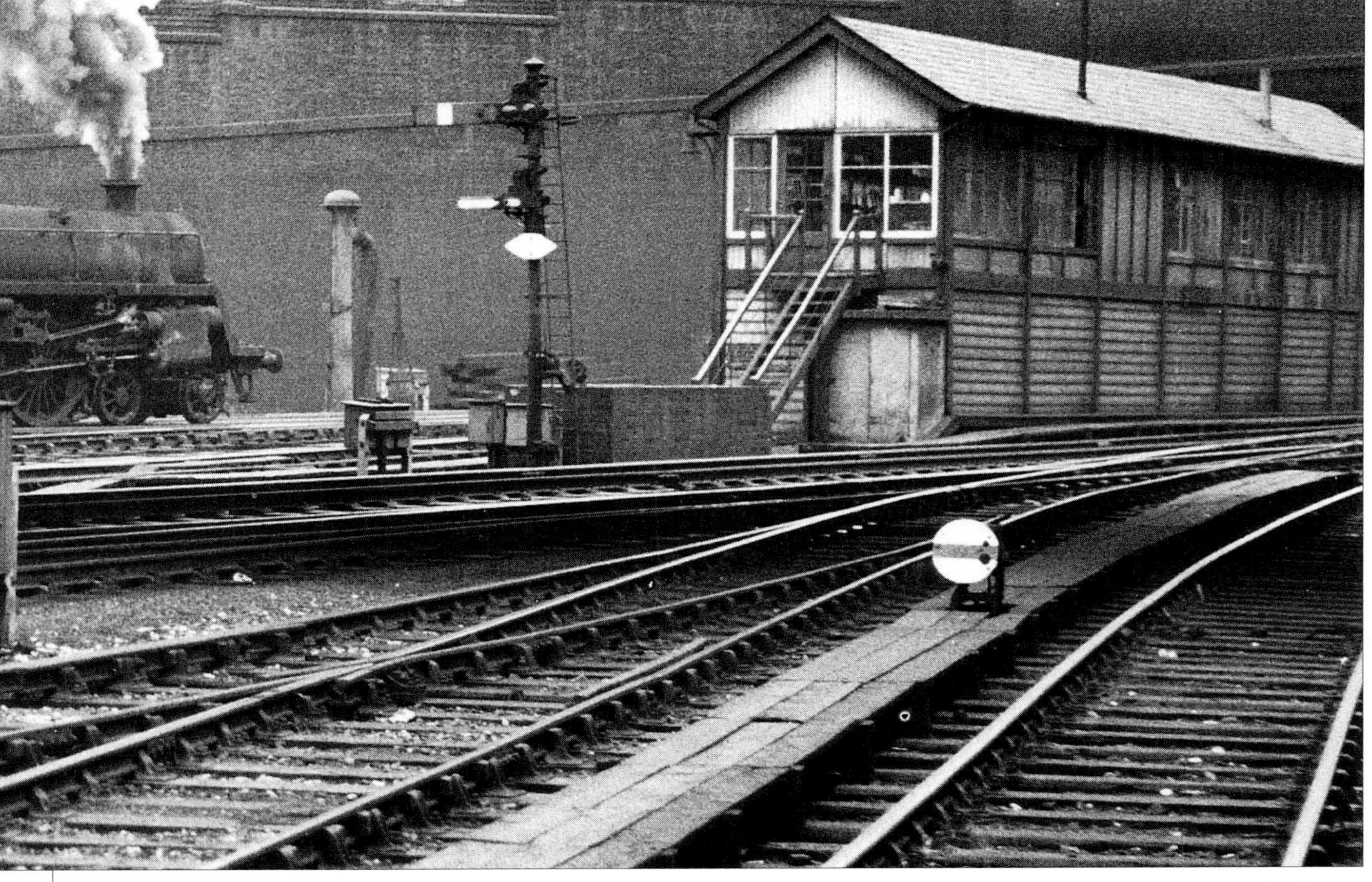

Down at the far end of Platform 1A under the concrete mass of the Hill Street bridge, the view is over to the Midland lines, where Standard Class 4 4-6-0 75004 is laboriously climbing out with the 4.35pm to Gloucester (Eastgate) on 15 April 1961. The big No.5 signalbox on the right controlled both Western and Midland lines at this end of the layout.

When I started work in 1949 near the city centre, I was able for two years to spend part of my lunch hour at New Street, just watching the goings-on. It was an 'open' station, meaning that one didn't have to undergo the usual scrutiny by a ticket-collector. The drawback was that, because tickets had to be collected on all inbound trains at places like Dudley Port and Saltley, unnecessary time was added to passengers' journeys.

I wasn't a well-informed railway enthusiast in those days – merely a fascinated onlooker. What I witnessed, though, certainly caused my interest in railways generally to develop. I was usually on the 12 o'clock lunch turn, when I could see the arrival at Platform 9 of the 'Pines Express', usually with a Longsight rebuilt Patriot or Scot, which would be detached. Meanwhile, the 10-10 ex-Sheffield had arrived at 12-16 behind a Midland Division Class 5, which had stood with the first coach of its train waiting to take the 'Pines' forward. When it had coupled up, everyone watched anxiously as this lesser engine, with its load of ten or eleven coaches, tackled the sinuous climb at 1 in 75/80 through the murky tunnels to Church Road. That task called for extreme skill on the part of the footplatemen, subject as they were to a degree of luck regarding the state of the engine, coal quality and atmospheric conditions.

Many a time a bout of slipping in the tunnel would result in the ensemble coming to a halt and having to set back into the platform and start all over again, sometimes with the assistance of the station pilot – usually a Midland 2P 4-4-0 on that side of the station. If the train engine driver was less confident, or knew the load was beyond his mount's official allowance for that daunting uphill start, he would request banking assistance in any case. In retrospect, it seems astonishing that so much was left to chance or individual initiative and skill. It also reminds me how relatively lightly-used were the tracks in and out of New Street in the 1950s. After the 'Pines's' 12-42 departure, on the Bristol route there was only a 12-50 stopper to Ashchurch via Redditch before the next train – a Bradford-Bristol at 1-23; so ten minutes wasted with a train stuck in the tunnel had little effect on following traffic. My notes from 1951, though, record that the 'Pines' seldom left New Street punctually.

By contrast at Platform 7, with a downhill entry and exit, the Bristol-Newcastle departure at 12-48 was a fairly straightforward operation. Almost always a Jubilee worked this and about the only untoward event would be a drawing-forward: always a difficult and time-consuming manoeuvre at this rather short, curved, crowded platform. If I had arrived early enough, I could also see the 12-15 local to Worcester setting off, usually behind a Compound 4-4-0 in those days.

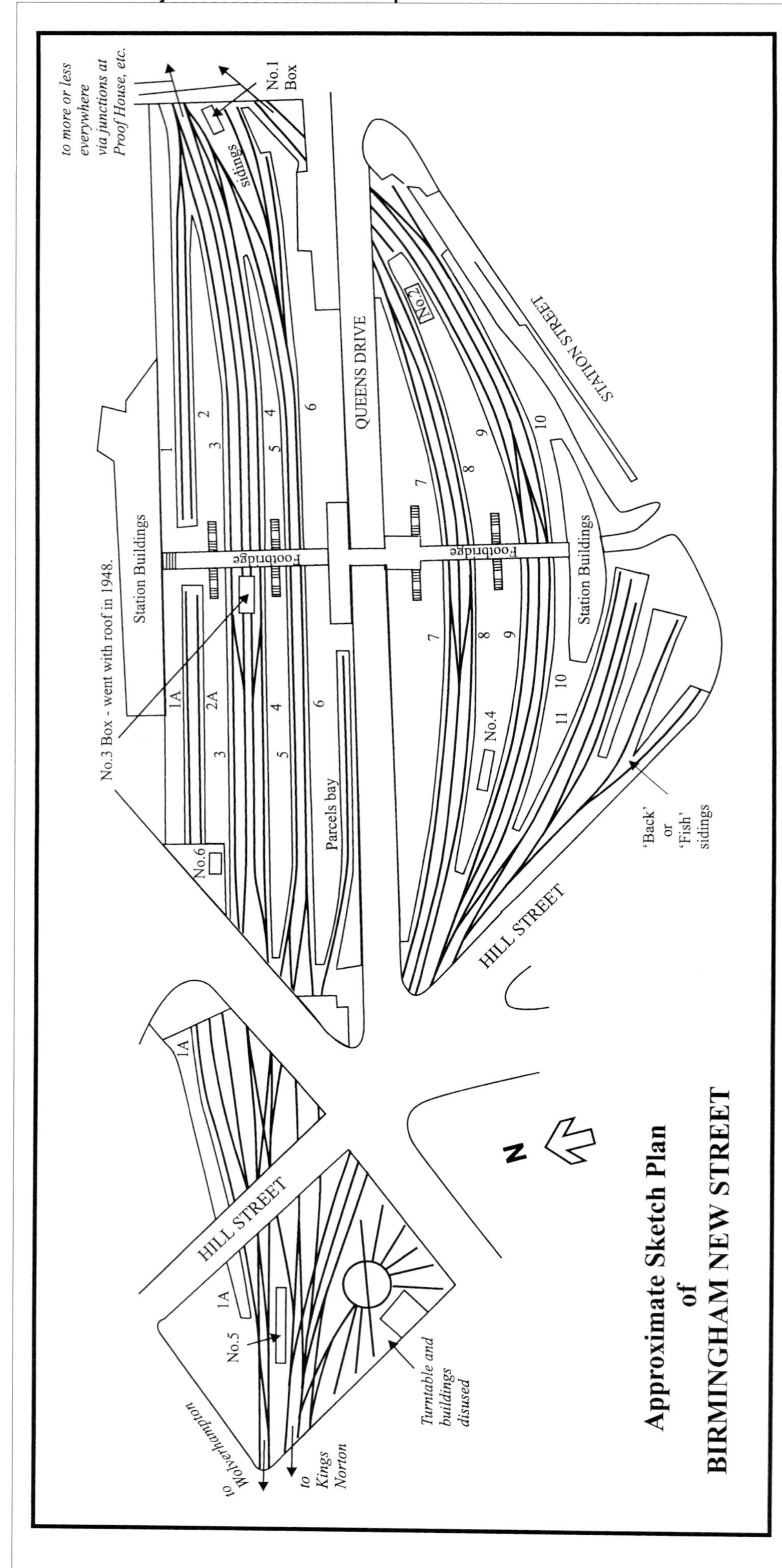

The scene over on the LNWR side, without the overall roof, was a great contrast, and the train workings also were very different. The LMS had come to the end of its existence in 1948, but the Western Division was still quite distinct from the Midland with its own locomotives and some operating practices inherited from Pre-Grouping days. The 12-40 departure for Euston (12-5 from Wolverhampton) was almost invariably a Royal Scot working (and quite a few of them were still not rebuilt at that time).

Following that train at Platform 3 would be the 10-15 from Liverpool and 10-20 from Manchester, combined at Crewe as usual and terminating at 12-50. Usually a Class 5 would be allocated to these medium-distance trains but with the number and variety of larger 4-6-0s available on the WCML, a Scot, Patriot or Jubilee was always possible. If I didn't have to be back at work on the dot of 1 o'clock, I might also see the arrival of the 6-17 ex-Lowestoft via Rugby: probably a Class 5 again.

There were local workings too, but my memory of those is surprisingly vague. We have all, I suppose, tended to take more notice of the heavier, faster or more glamorous trains... There were trains to Walsall, Wolverhampton and Coventry, many of them continuing to Rugeley, Stafford and Rugby respectively and serving such long-forgotten stations as Brindley Heath, Gailey or Brandon & Wolston. They were probably handled mostly by the 2-6-4 tanks, but a Midland 4-4-0 would not have been unlikely.

The station pilot on the LNW side in my earlier days of observation was an LNW 0-6-2 'Passenger Tank' – 46906 I think. Both this and the subsequent 'Coal Tanks' seemed incredibly primitive and antiquated machines but they did their mostly light and intermittent tasks well enough, following many decades of active service. Occasionally, when one of them had to draw half-a-dozen coaches into the east end tunnel and then propel them laboriously back into the station, I heard that rasping bark which would have been so familiar in the days when they were really made to work for a living!

One of several views which I took from Hill Street, this one on 15 April 1961 looks across to the Midland side of the layout, with the old turntable pit and some of its redundant spurs visible on the right. That site was occupied by the new signalbox when the station was rebuilt. A pair of later-type 'Derby Lightweight' DMUs is drawing out from Platform 7 or 8, after working in as the 3.30pm from Redditch. The steps of No.5 signalbox can be seen at bottom right.

Looking back now over about fifty years and helped by rough notes made at the time, I am constantly amazed at how the railways have been transformed – along with most other aspects of life of course. The dense fogs which we used to suffer every winter are virtually unknown now, for example; again and again my notebooks record the widespread delays from that cause. A good proportion of travellers in those days of National Service were in uniform. Then I recall the hundreds of staff required for the routine operations at New Street. The signalling was of LNWR design in both parts of the station and was operated by five signalboxes, four principal and one minor. An essential but unglamorous service was rendered by a squad of 'shunters' down on the tracks, who acted as mobile eyes to assist the signalmen. One of their methods of communication was a small metal trumpet, giving coded short and long blasts quickly

A scene from Platform 1A on a very murky, damp 30 January 1960. LMS 3F 0-6-0 tank 47494 is standing almost under Navigation Street bridge (Hill Street is the one beyond) on station pilot duty. Just behind and to the left of the camera position, in the gloom, was the smallest of the station's signalboxes.

A Gloucester RC&W 2-car DMU departs from Platform 2 on 18 June 1960 as the 7.40am to Coventry. Platform 1 is on the right and on the left, at Platform 3, a rebuilt Scot 46115 SCOTS GUARDSMAN has arrived with an express from the Crewe direction.

conveying instructions about when to switch points etc. If one of these men should read this, it would be interesting to know more about this system and other aspects of their job.

Constantly buzzing about the platforms were the petrol tractors, moving parcels and mailbags from one part of the station to another, on strings of platform trolleys. To my eyes, being used to the heavy, more solid GWR type with brakes, these trolleys were quite light and primitive. They did the job though, if rather noisily as the drivers took them to the limits of safe speeds. I don't recall any serious mishaps, which seems amazing considering the obstacles and passengers to be manoeuvred round, sometimes with half-a-dozen or more trolleys in tow. There were inclined ramps from each platform leading down to the interconnecting subway system through which this significant traffic passed. The Post Office had its own fleet of battery-powered tractors to share in the movement of mails about the station too.

There were porters (naturally with an eye to the more well-heeled travellers), platform inspectors, carriage examiners, booking clerks, catering staff, administrative and control personnel (mostly hidden from sight of course), parcels staff – and so on. Overseeing all this was the Station Master, seldom seen except on ceremonial occasions, ensconced just off the footbridge at the southern edge of the station.

We mustn't forget the station announcer, positioned high above Platform 7 and doing a remarkably efficient job of transmitting train information, instructing passengers 'to stand clear while the train draws forward' etc and summoning individual railwaymen quickly to sort out minor operational problems at specific points. I particularly remember the tricky matter of controlling the passengers thronging Platform 6, often used for originating departures for Liverpool and Manchester. The shortness of that platform meant that a normal train of ten or so coaches would, on arrival as empty stock from Vauxhall, have to draw through the platform to enable its tail end to clear the tracks at adjacent Platforms 5 (especially) and 4. That is assuming that there was a clear route at the west end of the platform, of course, because the next move was to set back the last two or three coaches into the extension bay at the east end. Thus the train could come to a halt twice before reaching its final departure position and each time passengers had to be dissuaded from boarding it, thereby hampering the operation. The platform staff liaised closely with the announcer, who was completely out of sight of Platform 6, to make carefully-timed and repeated injunctions to people. The good old-fashioned telephone there, given a handful of alert staff, was as efficient as present-day communication!

Another sign of how things have changed comes with the recollection of the number of extra trains regularly run as necessary in summer and at Bank Holidays – whenever there was pressure on the services. Boards were posted up around the station giving advance information of these trains, often running ahead of a heavily-used long-distance service, to relieve it of some overburden. Another strategy was to divide the Liverpool and Manchester trains into separate workings, incidentally saving those minutes wasted in splitting them at Crewe. In those days, of course, there was spare coaching stock standing about in sidings for this type of contingency; locomotives and crews, too, could be rustled up from the reduced freight activities at such times...

By the time of my first camera experiments, the scene had changed only slightly. The LNWR station pilots and Midland Class 3 4-4-0s had gone, but the pictures herewith show a scene changing only slowly at first. A quite disproportionate number of my New Street photographs, by the way, were taken on Saturday afternoons, due to the constraints of my working day. I crave readers' indulgence, therefore, as to any discrepancies between their personal memories and my own faithful record of the scene!

On the Midland side of the station where the platforms were still gaslit, the roof structures survived, in

The 1.48pm Wolverhampton (High Level) to Euston awaits departure time from Platform 3, double-headed by Stanier Class 5 4-6-0 45388 and Jubilee 45738 SAMSON. Platform 4 was my viewpoint, including No.1 signalbox on the right, on 27 September 1958. A year later, the fast Euston trains were virtually eliminated in order to reduce track occupation in connection with pre-electrification works. The GW Wolverhampton-Paddington route benefited from an enhanced service, compensating in some degree.

On 20 September 1956 coach roofboards were still the order of the day on most regular long-distance trains. Jubilee 4-6-0 45740 MUNSTER sets off at 12.30pm from Platform 3 at the head of the 11.55 Wolverhampton (High Level)-Euston.

increasingly decrepit condition, until 1964, by which time the bays at the north side of the station had been made into two long through platforms. This then enabled the LNW side to accommodate most existing traffic while Queen's Drive was obliterated and the Midland side totally rebuilt into its present form, with the LNW half following in time for the 1967 commencement of Euston electric services.

I briefly mentioned the low utilisation of tracks out of New Street on the Bristol route and a comparison with today is very revealing. Then, once beyond King's Norton the passenger service had priority in the competition for track space with an endless stream of slow-moving freight traffic – much of it coal. Now freight is a very minor factor in train movements. I have checked the number of departures from New Street between 0600 and 2300 in the Bristol direction in the 1950/51 winter timetable and find the total was just twenty-eight trains: ten long-distance, nine locals to or via Worcester and nine locals to Redditch or Ashchurch. That compares with an astonishing total, exactly fifty years later, of 119 (49 to Worcester or beyond, operated by three different companies, and 70 to Redditch). In 1951 the idea of an

On Good Friday, 4 April 1958, Stanier 2-6-4T 42560 has just arrived at Platform 3 with the 7.17am ex-Rugeley via Walsall. It is facing east because this train travelled via the Soho loop and Monument Lane and would, on an ordinary weekday at least, then continue to Coventry. The back of the Queen's Hotel rises up above all.

The familiar scene from the east end of Platform 6, looking across to Platform 3 where the motive power is more unusual. LMS Co-Co diesel electric 10000, one of 'the twins' is working the 1.55 Wolverhampton-Euston on 1 December 1956. The locomotive was in green livery by this time, and carrying the later BR crest. The rear view of the Queen's Hotel above is impressive if less than beautiful, and on the left the distinctive shape of an original 'Derby Lightweight' DMU is visible. These units worked most of the Sutton Coldfield locals for a couple of years until 1958.

electric service to Redditch would have been absurd: it was only a small market town then, with light manufacturing industry.

It would of course have been physically impossible for the old New Street to handle anywhere near that number of movements. When the rebuilding eventually started in 1963 it was long overdue because the structure was neglected and squalid. Whatever one's regrets about the austere concrete replacement at least it was functional and gave increased capacity. Now, however, after only thirty-three years or so, the place has become a byword for claustrophobic congestion and inconvenience, due to the huge increase in passenger usage and number of trains. How this problem may be resolved is a matter to tax many brains; ultimately, no doubt a compromise will be thrashed out, dependent on conflicting interests and available finance. The reopening of Snow Hill and re-siting of Moor Street stations in 1987 go only a little way to addressing the overall problem.

In about 2030, will someone write nostalgically about New Street Station at the turn of the 21st Century?

Arriving at Platform 3 on 22 September 1962 is BR/Sulzer Bo-Bo (later class 24) diesel-electric D5009. This class was fairly common on the lighter trains on the Western Division from 1960, including the Peterborough services via Market Harborough. In this case the working is the 12.15pm ex-Liverpool (Lime Street). Such views from the footbridge steps to the platforms are quite rare, due to the jostling of passengers!

In weak, wintry sun on 16 January 1960, Stanier Class 5 44867 is shunting empty stock at the west end of Platform 3, overshadowed by the Navigation Street Bridge.

Looking west, this is the space between Platform 4 (left) and Platform 3, with one track occupied by Stanier Mogul 42957 on a motley train of empty stock on 10 May 1957. An original 'Derby Lightweight' DMU stands at Platform 4 for one of the rush hour locals, under the cross station footbridge. Its utilitarian roof was fitted when the vast overall structure was removed in 1947. At Platform 3 the daytime train from Glasgow and Edinburgh has recently arrived.

This is the extension at the far east end of Platform 6 where on 18 February 1961, diesel shunter D3840 is depositing a van. There are a couple of other very short sidings on the left, usually holding an open wagon or two as rubbish receptacles; No.1 box is just out of the frame to the left. Many people will recognise this location as a spotters' Mecca where trains could also be glimpsed on the Midland lines – a small band of these devotees is evident on the right. Occasionally, when they became too numerous or rowdy, station staff would herd them away!

On 28 August 1958, Stanier 2-6-4T 42616 arrives at Platform 5 with the 5.15pm ex-Rugeley (Trent Valley). By a rare chance, Ivatt Class 4 2-6-0 43036 was captured also, leaving on the Midland line with another local. No.1 signalbox roof can just be discerned above the Rugeley train.

On 21 June 1958, not long after these units took over the Sutton Coldfield line workings, a 3-car Metro-Cammell DMU (with a 3-car Birmingham RCW set in multiple) leaves Platform 5 as the 4.08pm to Lichfield City. A bit of interesting signal detail can be studied, attached to the platform canopy support. The gentleman nonchalantly posing for the camera is unknown!

My only photograph of this piece of early diesel locomotive history was recorded on 12 March 1955: one of my earliest acceptable efforts. Built for the LMS by the North British Loco Co. with BTH electrical equipment, it was a Bo-Bo diesel-electric of only 827hp. It was thus not too suitable for other than fairly light trains, and was soon withdrawn when the 1955 Modernisation Plan started producing other designs. Here 10800 has just arrived at Platform 5 with the 6.35am from Yarmouth.

Looking out westwards from Platform 6 on 14 August 1958. Black Five 45091 stands under the stark girders of the 1948 replacement for the roof in the North Western half of the station. The train, at Platform 5, has just arrived as the 5.39pm ex-Rugby (Midland).

Rugby Black Five 44771 passes No.1 signalbox to arrive at Platform 6, heading the 7.02am ex-Yarmouth (Vauxhall) on 28 October 1961. Spotters are grouped at the end of Platforms 4/5 and another Black 5 is at Platform 3.

This was 11 February 1961 when diesels and electrics were still innocent of yellow warning panels. EE Type 4 D306 (later 40 106) waits to leave Platform 6 with the 3.50pm to Manchester Piccadilly. This class more or less took over the West Coast Main Line passenger workings from 1961 until electrification, and the distinctive whistling sound mixed in with their throaty growl is now but a happy memory.

Double-heading the 2.00pm to Liverpool and Manchester, mainly because of the climb through tunnel to Monument Lane, Crab 2-6-0 42814 and Jubilee 45567 SOUTH AUSTRALIA on 5 May 1958. The train is standing at Platform 6 and the viewpoint No.5, where a couple of platform trolleys are untidily parked.

Jubilee 45567 SOUTH AUSTRALIA is single-handed on this occasion, on the 2.0pm to Liverpool Lime Street, 10 March 1958. She is at the usual Platform 6 for such departures.

The west end of Platform 6 is the setting for a double-headed 2.0pm departure for Liverpool and Manchester, on 10 January 1957. Fairburn 2-6-4T 42674 is about to help Patriot 45539 E.C. TRENCH up the hill to Monument Lane.

The text refers to the complicated operations at Platform 6 for originating departures, and this was the scene on 5 May 1962. At this date the 2.00pm departure had became 1.45 for Liverpool and Manchester (by now Piccadilly) and all schedules were lethargic due to the engineering works in preparation for electrification. Having run through the platform for some distance, the driver is now cautiously backing the train in so that its tail coaches will occupy the extension at the east end, thereby making most of the train accessible to passengers. The engine is rebuilt Patriot 45526 MORECAMBE AND HEYSHAM.

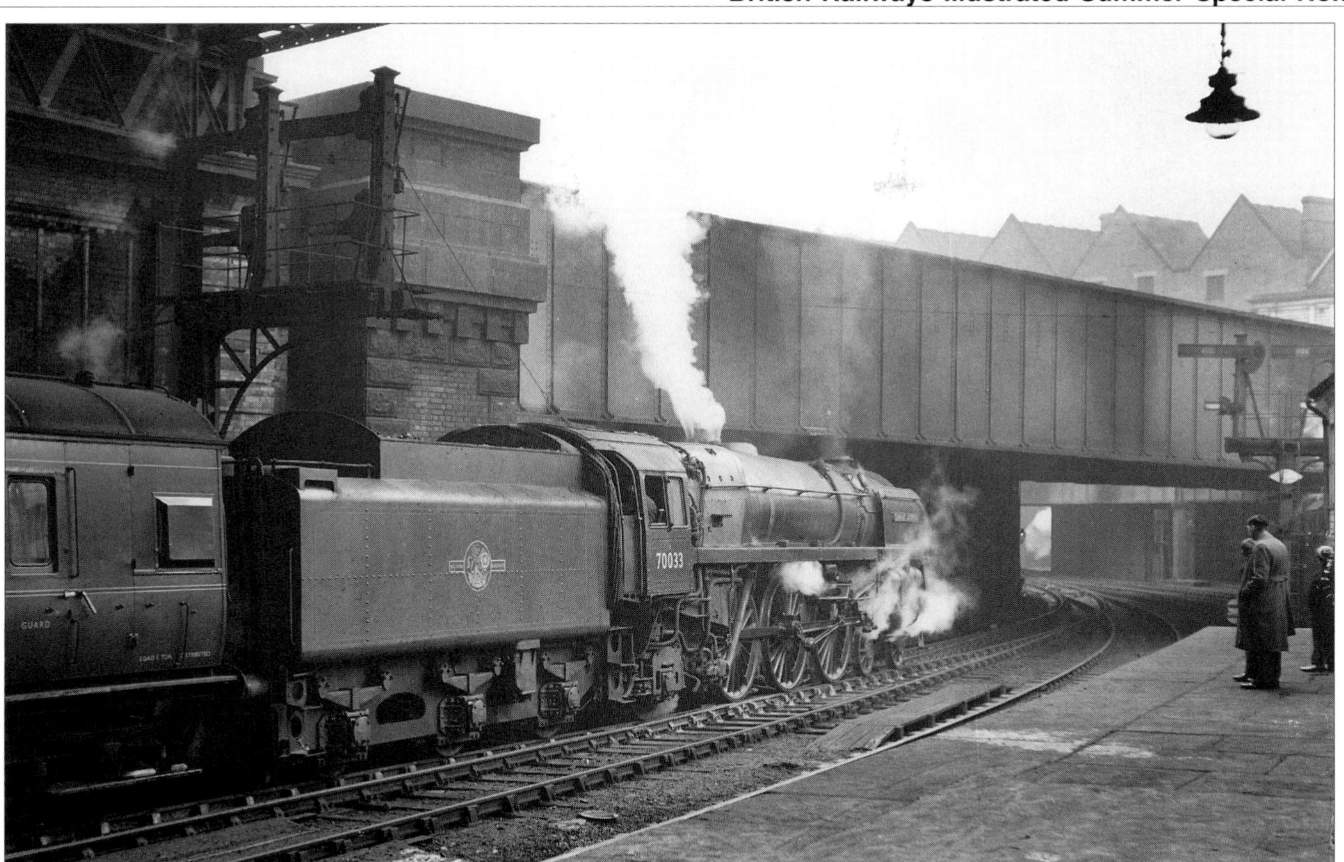

Western Division locomotives were not normally to be seen on the Midland side of New Street station. A regular exception was provided by 'The Pines Express' which changed engines here. On 8 November 1958, at Platform 7, Britannia Pacific 70033 CHARLES DICKENS has just taken over the northbound 'Pines' from a Midland Division engine, to work onwards to Manchester and Liverpool. At the rear of the train, by the way, Midland 2P 4-4-0 40443 had just removed the through Sheffield coach to be attached to the following 'Devonian'.

Production series Peak (later class 46) D154 arrives at Platform 7 on 23 June 1962 on what appeared to be the northbound 'Pines Express'; certainly it was labelled for Liverpool and Manchester. This being a Saturday, the 'Pines' was scheduled to run via Camp Hill and avoid New Street, so this could have been an extra train or an unexplained diversion.

The scene from the east end of Platform 10, near the parcels office. A Cravens 3-car DMU, the usual motive power for these services, leaves Platform 9 as the 3.15pm to Leicester (London Road) and Nottingham (Midland) passing No.2 signalbox, on 15 April 1961.

Mailbags typically litter the scene on Platforms 9 (left) and 10 (right) on 18 April 1958. The rubber-tyred trolley in the foreground is one of the Post Office type, but those on Platform 10 are the standard LMS pattern. LMS 4P Compound 4-4-0 41083 is awaiting departure on the 5.45pm 'parliamentary' stopping train to Bristol. The brackets at top left support No.4 signalbox.

The end of Platform 9 on Saturday 11 July 1959; it was not uncommon at this time to see a couple of 4Fs here on passenger trains. Sporting express headlamps at Platform 10 is Canklow's 44206 with the 12.15pm Scarborough-King's Norton, while more venerable ex-MR 43853 (of Gloucester shed) will follow on the 5.10 to Evesham and Ashchurch.

On 8 July 1961 Peak D94 (later class 45) is quite a focus of attention as she leaves Platform 9 with the 12.52pm York-Bristol. These locomotives were still fairly new at the time and were spreading from the St. Pancras route onto the cross-country services, where they survived for many years, building up something of a cult following.

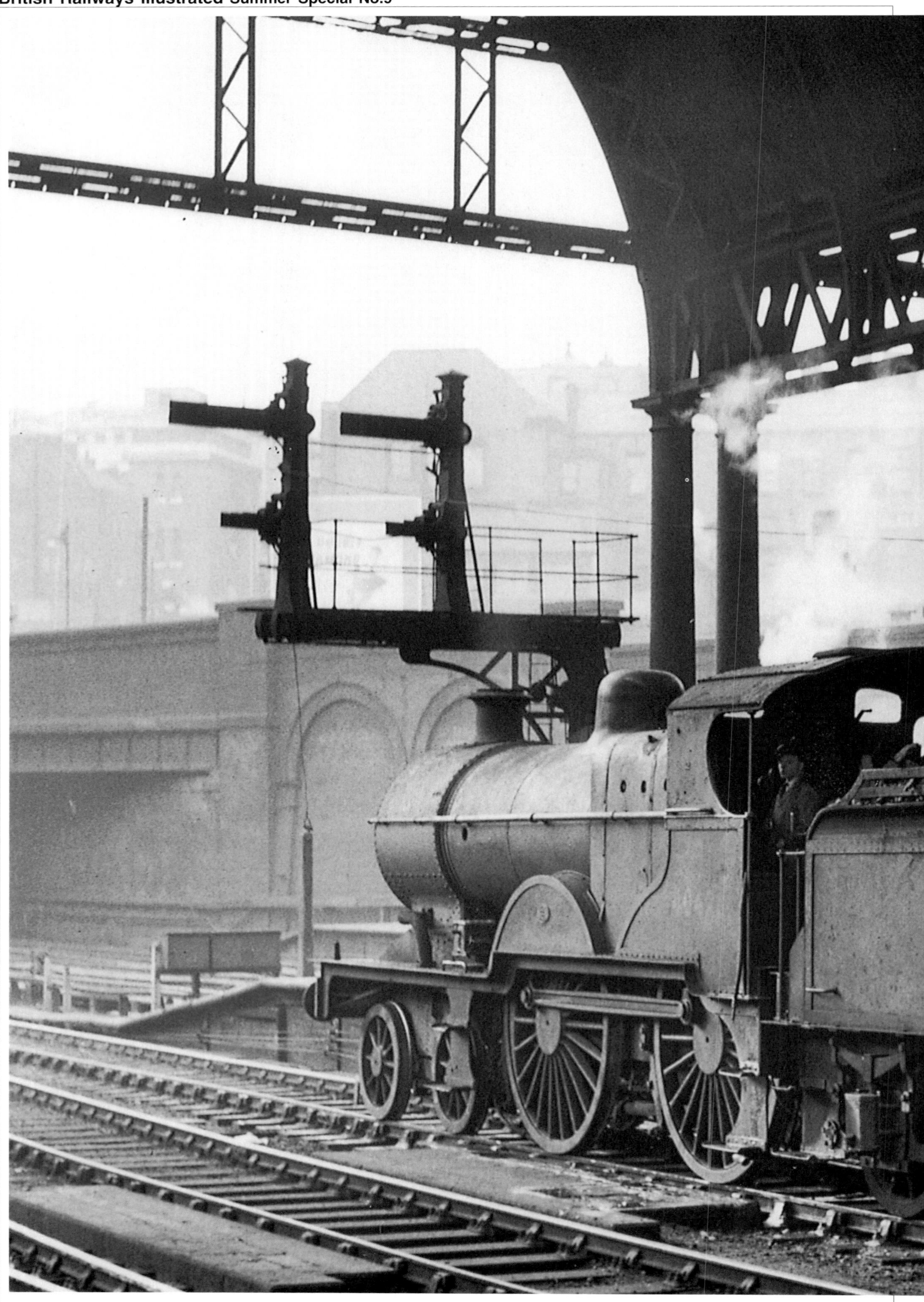

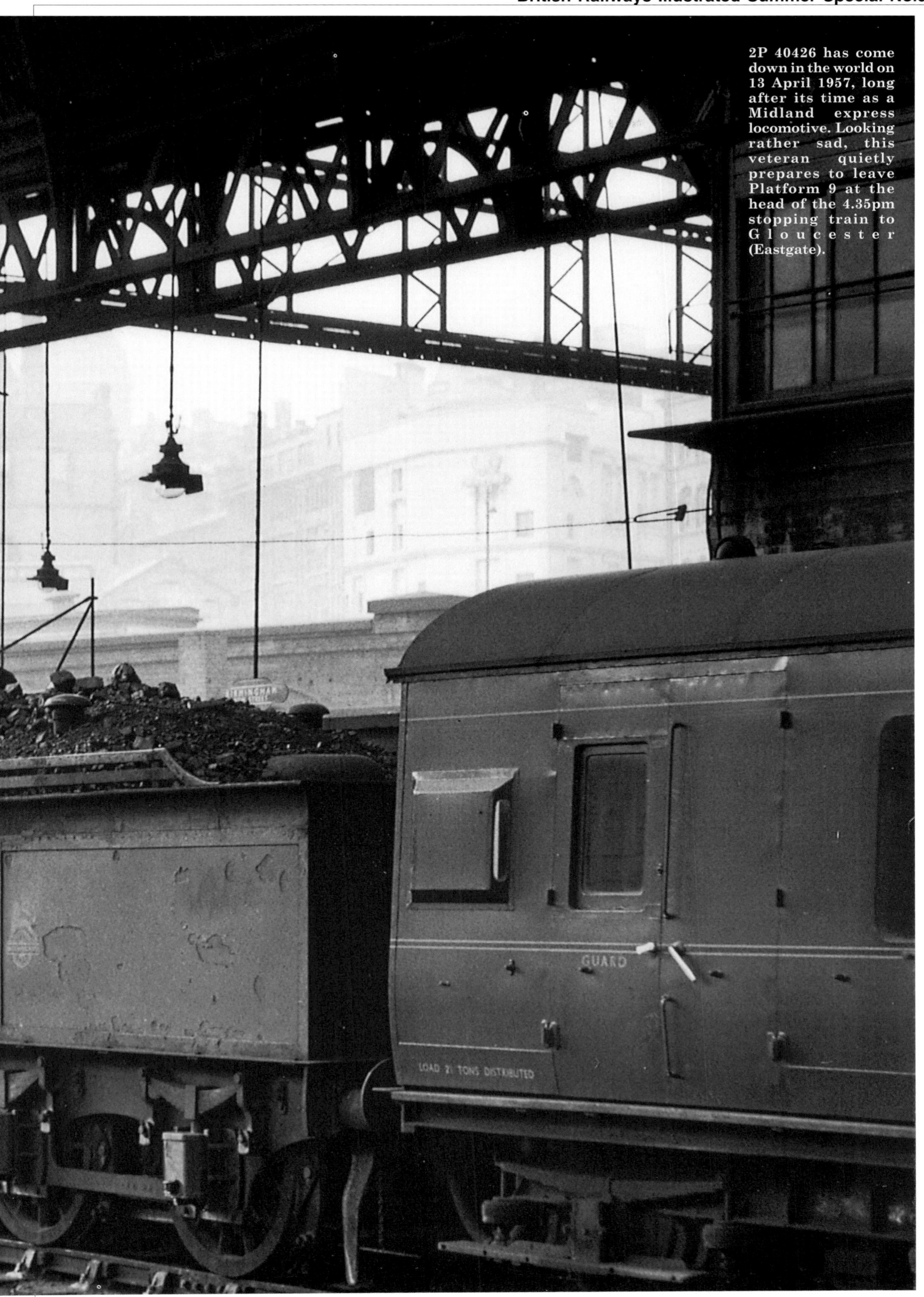

2P 40426 has come down in the world on 13 April 1957, long after its time as a Midland express locomotive. Looking rather sad, this veteran quietly prepares to leave Platform 9 at the head of the 4.35pm stopping train to Gloucester (Eastgate).

A familiar scene from Platform 10 as another northeast-southwest express prepared to tackle the climb to Church Road from No.9. On this occasion B1 4-6-0 61041 is piloting Jubilee 45579 PUNJAB on the 8.00am Newcastle-Cardiff, on 18 June 1960.

I travelled home on this train from Scarborough, the 12.15pm to King's Norton, on 2 August 1958. The 9F 2-10-0s quite often found good use on passenger services on summer Saturdays, and could achieve very respectable speeds. In fact, my expectations had been unduly raised by reports of their recent exploits when this one, 92118 of Westhouses, took over at Rotherham. I was disappointed – no fireworks on this occasion!

The original LMS Class 4 2-6-4Ts were one of the most successful designs produced in the directionless early period of the company's locomotive policy. Stanier of course restyled it, but the basic dimensions were retained and the Fowler version survived alongside the later ones. No.42327 awaits departure from Platform 10 on 2 April 1960 with the 4.10pm to Redditch. More mailbags lying around...

From the loading bay in the 'Back Sidings', an unusual viewpoint is presented here as a Birmingham RC&W 2-car DMU sets off from the short Platform 11, forming the 1.40pm to Redditch. By this date, 4 August 1962, the 350hp 0-6-0 diesel shunter was fairly common on pilot duties (this one was D3168).

To the Sunny Sout

The posters and publicity for the average British holiday in the 1950s and the first part of the 1960s promised a sort of wonderland that seems hopelessly overstated to us now. Yet they certainly didn't seem grotty, grainy places to us then. Even the journey was all part of the delight, whether by train (in musty stock just out of winter store, hauled by an 0-6-0 normally on coal work) or car, six or seven of you crammed in a Ford Pop. It could take all day to get to Hayling Island from north London in 1959 – which included of course, the statuary stops to replace a flat tyre, then a top hose. Hols then (seldom

2 Well, it is the Summer Special...

more than a week) were simple pleasures taken in simple places and, as anyone who has endured the fallout of a European air traffic controllers' strike can attest, had an attraction that grew more and more in the recollection. None of these photographs are labelled, unfortunately, but they seem to date from the early 1960s and three, happily, identify themselves. The Schools, 30926 REPTON, is approaching Sandling Junction on its way to the coast. All photographs Gavin Whitelaw Collection.

SOUTHERN CRYSTAL BALL GAZING

D.W. Winkworth

The Q class of 0-6-0s was relatively young in 1946 having been built before the Second World War and at the end of 1955 would be about 15-20 years old. Here No.30531 heads a cattle train at Southampton on a chilly 16 December 1950. Photograph L Elsey.

Seemingly oblivious of the impending Transport Bill heralding the nationalisation of the country's railways, Southern Railway general manager Sir Eustace Missenden announced on 31 October 1946 plans for electrification of the main lines in Kent and secondary routes in Sussex which, in effect, would result in the abandonment of steam traction on the Eastern and Central Sections of the railway. The secondary and branch lines of these two sections not selected for electrification were to be worked by diesel electric traction. It was thought that the scheme would result in the reduction of the total stock of steam engines by about a thousand from 1,800 to 800 units.

Whether this proposal was made with the intention of influencing the debate on nationalisation is not clear. However, it would serve to point the way forward irrespective of the political situation. In the event the Transport Bill was published on 28 December 1946 and received royal assent on 6 August 1947 to become effective as an Act on 1 January 1948.

Prior to making his announcement Sir Eustace had instructed that a committee comprising the traffic manager, the chief mechanical engineer, and the electrical engineer with the deputy general manager as chairman report on the expected locomotive position at the end of 1955 by which date the scheme would be complete. The report was to be based on the Eastern and Central Sections of the railway being electrified or dieselised with steam traction operating those routes of the Western Section not already electrified. This meant that everything west but inclusive of the main line from Sturt Lane Junction (near Farnborough) to Southampton would remain steam worked plus Alton to Fareham, Alton to Winchester Junction and local lines between Cosham, Gosport, Eastleigh and Southampton. Additionally the cross-London freight services were to remain steam hauled. Coupled with this remit was the recommendation for the types and numbers of new stock necessary.

By late September 1946 the report was presented to the general manager. Section 1 listed the stock position as at 31 December 1945, exclusive of that on the Isle of Wight, which was to be considered separately at a later date pending a general examination of the island's railway. This listing gave a total of 1,815 steam locomotives (of which 1,152 were tender engines) having an average tractive effort (at 85 per cent boiler pressure) per engine of 20,815lb and an average age of 37.23 years.

Section 2 of the report gave the projected requirements to operate the Western Section and the cross-London freight traffic, the estimate being founded on the peak traffic requirements for 1939. The passenger tender type headed the list with 306 engines followed by 169 goods tender engines, 111 passenger tanks, 13 goods tanks, 49 shunting tanks and 29 dock shunting tanks. There were to be 15 goods tanks for the cross-London freight work so giving a total of 692 engines. Of the dock tanks 18 were allocated to Southampton Docks and 11 for Dover, Folkestone and Newhaven; it was considered necessary to keep steam for these docks instead of introducing diesel traction – a curious decision indeed.

'Selection of Locomotives' was the title of Section 3 of the report. As might well be expected the passenger tender type predominated with 271 units; this figure was made up of 20 Merchant Navy, 70 West Country, 16

Merchant Navy 1. The Merchant Navy class was the preferred express passenger locomotive and it was in this, the original form, that the Committee based their recommendation. 21C2 is at Exmouth Junction shed in 1949. It had gone into works in September 1949 and Eastleigh had not been able to bring itself to remove the big gunmetal cab and tender plates; they were not finally done away with until January 1950. Photograph James Stevenson, courtesy Hamish Stevenson.

Lord Nelson, 54 King Arthur, 40 Schools, 21 U1 class 2-6-0s and 50 U class (also 2-6-0s). Goods tender engines earmarked numbered 191 (although most of these did undertake some passenger work) of which there were 40 Q1 class 0-6-0s, 20 Q class 0-6-0s, 45 S15 4-6-0s, 80 N class 2-6-0s and six N1 class 2-6-0s. Existing E2 0-6-0Ts would account for 10 of the passenger tank complement of 35 and the remainder would be made up of new construction.

Goods tank engines selected numbered 24 of specialist nature; there were four G16 class 4-8-0Ts for Feltham hump shunting work, five class H16 4-6-2Ts and 15 W class 2-6-4Ts for cross-London freight traffic. Assessment of the shunting tanks revealed a motley collection of 23 engines led by eight Z class 0-8-0Ts, a couple of C14 class 0-4-0Ts, ten new construction plus the three diesel electric shunters engaged at Norwood yard on shunting duties which one would have thought should have remained there instead of being transferred to

Southern Railway £15,000,000 Electrification and Diesel Traction Scheme

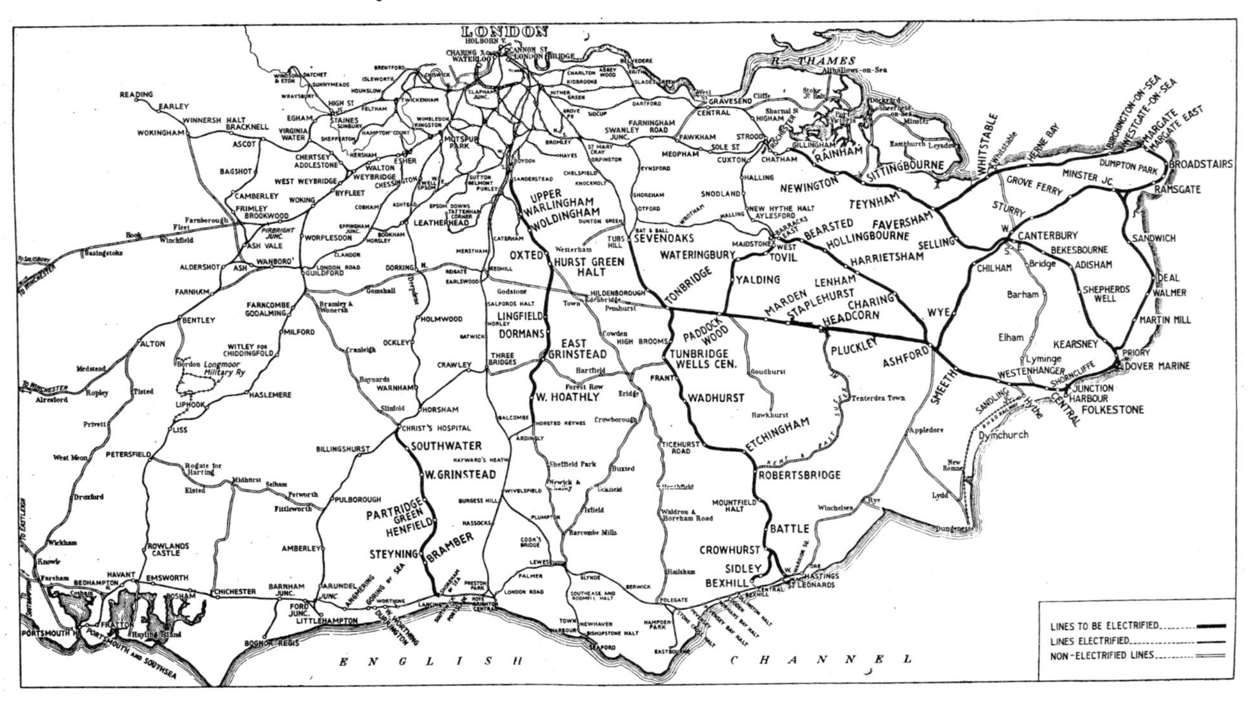

Map showing lines to be electrified under the 1946 Scheme.

Merchant Navy 2. One of the second batch of Merchant Navys (they were built in three batches of ten each) 35014 NEDERLAND LINE climbs out of Blackboy tunnel with an up train, 13 August 1954. Exmouth Junction concrete works is behind the sidings on the right. Photograph J. Robertson, The Transport Treasury.

the Western Section. This selection gave 544 units towards the 692 requirement throwing up a surplus of 22 goods tender engines and shortfalls of 35 passenger tender engines, 76 passenger tanks, 4 goods tanks, 26 shunting tanks and 29 dock shunting tanks. It was considered that if 30 new passenger tender engines – doubtless Pacifics – were to be built that would be sufficient of this type and the theoretical shortage of five could be disregarded. The twenty-two surplus goods tender engines were to be split; six N1 class 2-6-0s were to be converted to W class 2-6-4 tanks to counter the shortage of that class while the remaining 16 were to be considered as covering passenger tank duties but without conversion to such. Even so, the passenger tank stock still required 60 units which were to come from new construction (the expected Leader type). The goods tanks were now – again in theory – in surplus to the tune of two units which it was decided to disregard. The last two categories, shunting tank and dock shunting tank, were

Merchant Navy 3. 35007 ABERDEEN COMMONWEALTH at Exmouth Junction, 15 August 1957. Photograph W. Hermiston, The Transport Treasury.

Merchant Navy 4. In the period 1956-1959 all the Merchant Navy Pacifics were rebuilt into more conventional form, one probably somewhat to the surprise of some members of the Committee. This is 35020 BIBBY LINE at Waterloo, 8 July 1962. Photograph Alec Swain, The Transport Treasury.

to be brought up to the required strength with new construction.

The withdrawal of certain classes as being unsuitable for use after the end of 1955 was outlined in Section 4 of the report. Twenty of the earlier, Urie members of the King Arthur class were to go together with twenty H15 class 4-6-0s (poor steaming and high coal consumption). The seven Remembrance class (non-standard class of inadequate performance for post-1955) would go too, as well as life-expired M7 class 0-4-4 tanks (58 of those) and 25 B4 class 0-6-0 dock tanks. The L1 class 4-4-0s were based on a 1914 design and by end of 1955 there would be no suitable work available. The 17 K class 2-6-0s would be made redundant on the Central Section and there would be no suitable work for them on the Western Section and, in any case, the average age of the engines was not in their favour. Three engines built in 1907 for the Plymouth, Devonport and South Western Junction Railway were completely non-standard and life expired. No attempt was made to explain the demise of other classes, such as the T9 4-4-0s, because it was evident that their course had been run in terms of age. A list of class withdrawals was, nevertheless, appended. Of the stock of 1,818 locomotives no less than 1,359 were recommended for withdrawal, the average age of these (at the end of 1955), being 54.71 years.

Recommendations as to the retention and rebuilding of the steam stock were the subject of Section 5 of the report. It confirmed that the E2 class 0-6-0 tanks should be regarded as passenger tank engines rather than shunting engines and suggested that the six N1 class 2-6-0s should be rebuilt into W class 2-6-4 tanks, as recounted above.

Purchase of locomotives was considered next, in Section 6. It was noted that purchase of ten Ministry of Supply 0-6-0 tank engines was not to be proceeded with. Instead 14 0-6-0 ex-USA dock tanks were being acquired for working Southampton Docks. Also it was noted that 15 diesel shunting engines were under consideration as an addition to stock.

New construction was dealt with in Section 7. For the requirement of 35 modern express passenger engines 10 Merchant Navy and 20 West Country 4-6-2s were suggested. A case was made for the ten large Pacifics as being necessary on the grounds of:

(a) the necessity of adequate motive power to ensure good timekeeping
(b) the sustained trend towards weight increases in express passenger coaching stock
(c) the constant demand for accelerated express services and
(d) the reasonable expectation of heavy traffic on the Western Section main lines.

So far as the shortage of 60 passenger tanks was concerned, nothing other than a general, somewhat self-evident observation was made that the design should be able to conform, in weight and curvature restrictions, with the minor branch lines such as Wenford Bridge (although this was freight only) or Lyme Regis and could be steam or diesel. The same type of remark was made in respect of the shortage of shunting and dock shunting tanks; in the latter case small diesel locomotives were considered the most suitable answer.

If all the recommendations were carried out the average age of motive power units as at 31 December 1955 would be reduced to 19.09 years and the average tractive effort increased to 27,385lb. The withdrawal of the older engines would mean that the West Country class would have to work over the Brockenhurst to Bournemouth and Weymouth via Ringwood route, which was subject to a 30mph speed restriction for the class. It would be necessary to bring the line up to standards for normal

Merchant Navy 5. 35023 at Nine Elms, 13 August 1959. Photograph W. Hermiston, The Transport Treasury.

speeds at an estimated cost of £30,000. Likewise the Salisbury-Bournemouth via Fordingbridge route would cost £40,000.

There was a general qualification at the end of report thus:

'The Committee would emphasise the fact that the actual conditions as regards electrification in 1955 may, owing to a variety of circumstances differ considerably from those now assumed, and they point out the necessity of ensuring that whatever those conditions may be, the motive power, steam, diesel or electric, required to work the traffic either then or in the meantime, shall, in fact, be available. Should it so happen that the completion of the electrification of the Eastern and Central Sections be

Above and top right. **The case for the large Pacifics – adequate power to ensure good timekeeping – is demonstrated here with two pictures of the Bournemouth Belle. In one it is approaching Vauxhall in the down direction in Southern days, hauled by 21C19 FRENH LINE C.G.T. while in the other, in the BR era, it is leaving Waterloo in the charge of 35020 BIBBY LINE. This train, apart from the Devon Belle, was the heaviest worked on the Western Section lines. Both courtesy G. Goslin, Gresley Society.**

delayed beyond 1955, or that steam working requirements are greater than the 1939 peak, then it would be necessary to retain in service beyond the period contemplated by the Committee a number of the older steam locomotives or alternatively to build more new ones.'

It was very much a case of crystal ball gazing of course and so it is not surprising that some areas suffered from cloudiness. No mention had been made of the nationalisation of the railways and maybe it was thought that the Southern would carry on managing its own affairs. In the event that was true to an unexpected degree, such as day-to-day running. When it came to new projects, however, the region could recommend but not decide and so the electrification had to wait some years to gain approval and what had been foreseen to some degree in the

The light Pacifics were built as though there was no tomorrow. Seventy, judged necessary by the Committee, was a mere bagatelle ... eighty, ninety, one hundred on to one hundred and ten. Am I bid any more? All done at 110? A mere brace stand ready at Exmouth Junction shed to take over the two portions of the Devon Belle from Exeter Central. On the left, 34016 BODMIN will power the Ilfracombe portion while 34013 OKEHAMPTON is on duty 613, the Plymouth part of the service. Photograph H.C. Doyle, courtesy G.W. Goslin, Gresley Society.

No.34087 145 SQUADRON passing Bickley Junction on 16 July 1955 with the 12.10pm Ramsgate-Nottingham (Victoria) service. Photograph D.W. Winkworth.

qualification at the end of the report came true. The completion date got put back from 1955 to 1961. To some extent the traffic did exceed 1939 standards but this was offset by a larger number of light Pacifics being built.

Despite nationalisation the ten Merchant Navy engines got built and no less than 110 light Pacifics were produced (40 more than asked for in the report) before the flow could be staunched by BR headquarters. The passenger tank type was one that the Southern Railway never saw the need to modernise being content to use aged engines, such as the M7 and H 0-4-4 tanks or veteran 4-4-0s and never constructed a new design of this type throughout its existence. The proposal to use the ten E2 class on these duties never came to anything, although some of the surplus N class 2-6-0s might have done some of the work. It was the ill-fated 'Leader' which was supposed to fill this passenger tank role but

If the modified Merchant Navy class could not have been foreseen by the committee, similarly unthinkable was the notion of a rebuilt light Pacific. Here, 34066 SPITFIRE is contrasted with modified 34060 25 SQUADRON at Eastleigh. Photograph I. Laidlaw, The Transport Treasury.

The batches of King Arthurs built during the existence of the Southern Railway, numbering fifty-four, were selected by the Committee for the post-1955 era. Here No.30775 SIR AGRAVAINE passes through London Bridge on 23 June 1957 with a Ewer Street to Dover ferry van train. Photograph L. Elsey.

failed to come to fruition. Eventually LMR and BR designed 2-6-2 and 2-6-4 tanks were drafted in for the purpose.

The goods tanks never had their ranks swelled by six N1 class engines converted to 2-6-4 tanks; the Q1 class of goods tender type were the ones to fill that shortfall. The shunting and dock shunting tanks were ousted by diesel units.

It was a brave effort to try to forecast the position at electrification. The table indicates how successful they were.

STEAM STOCK TO BE RETAINED AFTER ELECTRIFICATION IN 1955

Locomotive Type	Report Proposal	Actual end 1955	Actual end 1961
Merchant Navy	30	30	30
West Country	70	110	110
Lord Nelson	16	16	10
King Arthur	54	54	12
Schools	40	40	25
U1 2-6-0	21	21	21
U 2-6-0	50	50	50
Q1 0-6-0	40	40	40
Q 0-6-0	20	20	20
S15 4-6-0	45	45	45
N 2-6-0	80	80	80
N1 2-6-0	0	6	6
E2 0-6-0T	10	10	6
G16 4-8-0T	4	4	2
H16 4-6-2T	5	5	5
W 2-6-4T	21	15	15
Z 0-8-0T	8	8	8
C14 0-4-0T	2	2	0

Although ungainly the Q1s were versatile machines working freight and passenger traffic as occasion arose. They were modern and powerful and were useful for cross-London freights as well as on the Hastings Direct line. 33002 plods along somewhere in the electrified area with a modest collection of freight vehicles in September 1959. Photograph The Transport Treasury.

Below. **Although all the Schools were active at the end of 1955 by the time electrification came to pass the class had been decimated – indeed more than strict decimation – with fifteen of them gone. 30919 HARROW leaves Groombridge on 14 May 1960 with a Tunbridge Wells West-Brighton service. Photograph D.W. Winkworth.**

The Southern Railway was rich in Moguls so that all eighty of class N were included in the steam stock to be retained after 1955. In this picture No.31830 is arriving at Mortehoe with the 1.10pm from Exeter Central, on 5 September 1959. Photograph D.W. Winkworth.

That unlovely but useful bulk once more; 33023 at Bournemouth shed on 24 July 1951. Given its outline, some have all-too casually dismissed the Q1s as a Bulleid 'eccentricity' but this is ignorant. The Q1 represented a 'formidable enhancement' (see E.S. Youldon's comprehensive account of the class in last year's *BRILL Annual #9*) over the existing SR 0-6-0, the Qs, and for less than two tons over the weight of the far smaller engines. Hence the pared down look; it wasn't eccentricity, it was clever stuff. Photograph The Transport Treasury.

The Southern had a policy of working branch lines with engines past their prime, hence the need in Bulleid's mind for a modern branch line engine – the 'Leader'. In the wake of nationalisation what happened was that new 2-6-2Ts of LMS design were sent in. No.41224 runs into Corfe Castle with the 14.10 Wareham-Swanage service on 20 May 1966. Photograph D.W. Winkworth.

Similarly, the LMS 2-6-4T design appeared on Southern metals in original form and, as here, in a BR adaptation. No.80043 forsakes its passenger role in favour of a ballast train just east of Eastleigh South Junction on 14 March 1961. Photograph L. Elsey.

30702
30702

SOUTHERN
88

Left. A lot of the old veterans lingered on long after, in theory, they should have gone, as for example T9 class 4-4-0 No.30702 which on 3 August 1957 was assisting (banking tender first was then a regular duty) the 10.25am Poole-Bradford (Exchange) service through Parkstone station up the bank to Branksome. Photograph D.W. Winkworth.

Below left. One of the Report's 'life-expired' B4 tanks, No.88 about 1946. Along with several of the class, 88 had lasted to the late 1950s (1959 in 88's case) and a handful more survived in use into the early 1960s. Photograph The Transport Treasury.

Below. Though selected for metamorphosis into W class 2-6-4 tanks the small N1 class never reached that stage. Because the U and N 2-6-0s could not meet clearance restrictions between Tonbridge and Bo-Peep Junction St Leonards the half-dozen three-cylinder N1s proved the answer. This is 31876 on a down Ramsgate relief at Denmark Hill, 16 May 1959. Photograph R.C. Riley.

Once Was Everyday...

A selection of once ordinary daily delights

By Paul Wilmshurst

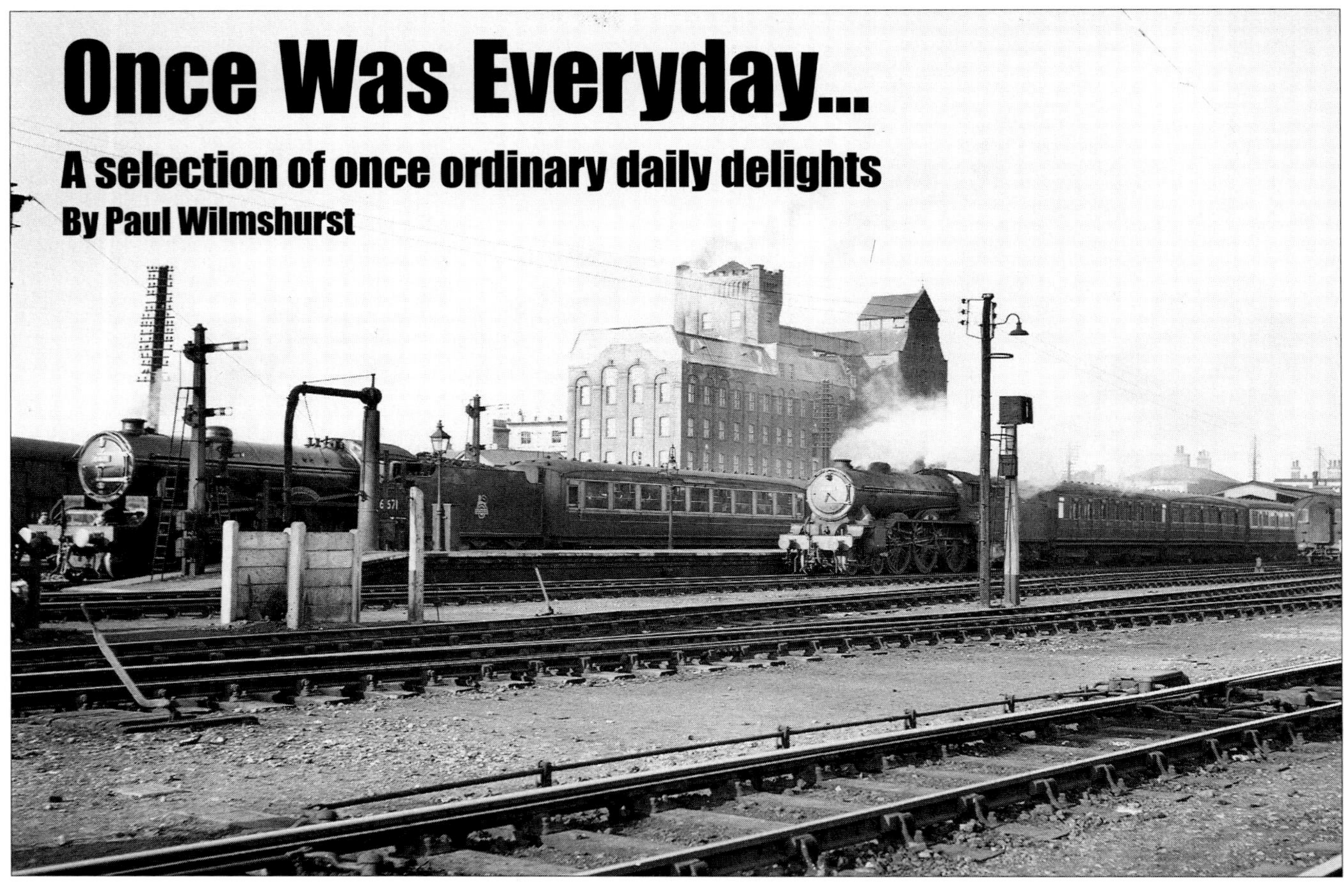

Dividing of the ways. B2 4-6-0 61671 ROYAL SOVEREIGN stands at Cambridge on 24 February 1953 with the 3.10pm for Kings Cross while B17 61653 HUDDERSFIELD TOWN waits on the main platform with the 2.55pm for Liverpool Street. For more of these once daily delights, see, of course, the article in this very volume, *The Gresley B17 and Thompson B2 4-6-0s*. On the extreme right is an E4 2-4-0 on station pilot work, No.62786. Photograph M.N. Bland, The Transport Treasury.

A rather more bucolic scene. In the 1950s (before 1957 anyway) 5911 PRESTON HALL (the shedplate looks like 86A, making it an Ebbw Junction engine) rolls into Newnham on the main line between Gloucester and Newport, in that border country part of Gloucestershire *west* of the Severn Estuary. It is the sheer *normality* of this scene, repeated as it was thousands of times across the country every day, that makes it so endearing. The very particular way everything is arranged – trolleys, luggage, smattering of staff, flower bed, goods shed and signal box – make it almost a template for preserved stations today. But that really is how it looked. Photograph M.N. Bland, The Transport Treasury.

Battle of Britain Pacific 34088 213 SQUADRON stands in full glory at Eastleigh shed, out by the back of the coal stage where at this time engines were more likely to be coaled by crane than from the old stage. Ex-works and unveiled in 'rebuilt' form that very day, 10 April 1960, the engine has literally travelled the short distance from the Works, a few yards away to the left, over Campbell Road. Preternaturally clean it has yet to receive any coal in that gleaming tender but, as soon as that initial bucket goes up, the first of very many fine dustings of coal will begin to coat 213 SQUADRON. Photograph Les Elsey.

And what on earth to make of this? The shed *habitué* (as we might call ourselves) would be used to 'roundhouses', from one end of the country to another, though they would all be much of a muchness; some vast and airy, others pokey and semi-derelict. There were oddities of course, strangely enough positioned at opposite ends of the country. There was an exotic semi-roundhouse at St Blazey in Cornwall and a riotously extravagant one at Inverness. If ever an industrial building deserved preservation, that was it. Sadly, it was not to be. Generally overlooked (again, scandalously unlisted – have you *seen* some of the rubbish that gets listed now?) was the old roundhouse at Stoke. It had long been superseded by a big straight shed (falling down by the 1960s) and was a backwater, given over to tanks and other engines small enough for its 50ft turntable. Its beauty was in the way it represented ancient thinking of a kind now long lost – it once had a *circular* lifting crane serving the roads for instance. Everything had a home at Stoke – the wooden building on the left was the breakdown crane shed. Beat that for 'everyday'... Photograph Paul Chancellor Collection.

Blue Train* to Anniesland

Forget that 'Sunny South' stuff; here's what we're all more used too, and likely enough to get too. These notes were made in March as the country was drenched yet again, though the long term forecast says this summer (2001) will be 'the best for five years'. Hmm. We'll see – most amusing letter concerning railways, rain and/or the met office received by 1 September 2001 wins a free year's subscription. The picture by the way (see *Glasgow Railway Memories*, Irwell Press, by Smith and Anderson – quote this article with your order and get it post free) is Airdrie in the drizzle, with V3 2-6-2T No.67618 waiting to leave with a substitute electric 'Blue Train' service, the 5.18pm to Anniesland, April Fool's Day, 1961. The three ladies, if they but knew, would be glad of the wind direction. Photograph W.A.C. Smith.

**This service has been temporarily suspended.*

Night Shapes

General dereliction followed by bombing left the district around Waterloo a sadly knocked about place. Early office development gobbled up much of the rubble, transforming the view with what, for the 1960s, was almost space age modernity. Even the box at Waterloo had 'the look', while the steam engines at the station looked increasingly out of kilter with their surroundings. The effect was heightened at night... Photographs Alistair Nisbet.

From Crewe to Swindon and Back

The first 8F, 8000, as outshopped in grey with highlights whitewashed for clarity, in 1935 – original power classification '7F'. 8000 has the original 'dome-less' boiler as fitted to the first twelve (books say only 8003 was provided with the later boiler, in order to provide a spare dome-less boiler for the rest of that batch 8000-8011 i.e. a 'float'). 8000-8011 were built without vacuum brake equipment (compare with the much later 8400) and were steam-brake only at first. Note the LNW red bricks of the Crewe wall under the boiler – a spot the photographic lab failed to 'blank' out.

As is well known, the 8Fs, as a *de facto* wartime standard, were built at Swindon, Doncaster, Ashford and so on. The rest of the pictures show the first of Swindon's efforts, 8400, in June 1943. Despite the War she had been prepared for the Official Photograph – but those cylinder and steam chest covers did not stay polished long! Note works plate LMS BUILT 1943 G.W.R. 8400 did not find its way 'home' to the LMS until after the war's end.

Perhaps the most interesting feature are the *dual* lamp brackets to suit both GWR and LMS standard lamps. How long did these last, you feel yourself wondering...The tender buffer beam has been drilled to take the bracket for a steam heating hose (they have been ringed in chalk). Perhaps it was done on an 'if ever required' basis. A few 8Fs were fitted for carriage warming – one was used at Willesden for instance to haul stored empty stock from Verney Junction ready for the summer 'peak'; it was a requirement that they be steam-heated on their way up to 'dry out' before re-entering traffic. These trains were made up to 20+ coaches, hence the 8F proved useful, 'saving' a much needed Black Five for something better!

8400 has the standard LMSR vacuum brake ejector in front of the cab, yet when some returned to the WR in later years they were modified with a GWR ejector just behind the smokebox. Ex-GWR drivers deplored the lack of vacuum pumps on these; 'wasting good steam' to maintain vacuum whilst running was NOT GWR practice! However, the Swindon 8Fs were intended eventually for general use. There is no smokebox number (Swindon Foundry would not have had the necessary patterns to hand) but apparently no painted number on the buffer beam. Perhaps they were added later but, there is a SDN shed code above the front step on both sides!

WORMIT, 1955

By Alistair F. Nisbet

at Tay Bridge South box. On account of these standard restrictions no specific restriction of speed over the curve in the tunnel had been imposed, although one has since been applied.

'Train working is by single line electric token instruments. In the Down direction branch line trains approaching the junction are controlled by two Home signals and a worked Distant signal. The Outer Home signal is 88 yards beyond the east end of the tunnel and the Distant is 584 yards beyond the home. The Distant can be seen from the right hand side of the footplate of an engine (in the direction of travel) at a distance of some 960 yards. It remains in view for 200 yards but is then obscured until it comes into view again at 540 yards. The signalman in Tay Bridge South box obtains a good sideways view, over the tunnel, of a Down train soon after it passes the Distant signal'.

The day was hot, the sky clear with a moderate easterly wind and the rails were dry. Soon after the accident Colonel McMullen had thoroughly checked the track and found it to be well maintained.

Two excursions had been run to the Tayport branch that day; train No.120 had left Dundee Tay Bridge at 1.35pm and arrived at Tayport at 2.00pm while a second, No.121, had left at 2.05pm for East Newport and arrived at Tayport as empty stock at 2.32pm. By this time the engine from No.120 had run round its stock and disposed it in Dixon's siding, near to Tayport South Signal Box.

A similar run round movement had taken place for No.121 and it too was left in a siding between the station and the South Signal Box. Such movements were necessary as there was insufficient siding space at East Newport; it was also necessary to keep the running lines clear at Tayport to allow the through service for St Andrews to pass to Leuchars and the engine of the various Tayport-only local service to perform its run round manoeuvres. Subsequent events at Tayport had a direct and crucial bearing on how and why the accident occurred, as we shall see.

The return working of No.121 was due to leave Tayport for East Newport as ECS train No.122 and originally had been scheduled to depart at 6.00pm but this was later altered – how and why is not clear. In the event it did not actually get underway until 6.24pm. The working instructions had included a requirement for the locos to be exchanged between trains at Tayport but this did not happen, again for reasons unexplained, and the crews returned on their original mounts.

Train No.123 (the return working of No.120) should have departed at 6.53pm – all passengers were supposed to be aboard by 6.45pm, after which the train would shunt back out of the Down platform as far as the Home signal to allow a service train due at 6.51pm to enter the Up platform. However, No.123 did not enter the Down platform until 6.42pm and stopped halfway along at the Home signal; some passengers were able to join the leading three or four coaches. Once the Up service had arrived two drawing-up movements took place to ensure that all carriages could be loaded safely. Departure was eventually achieved at 7.01pm.

Train No.123 was not booked to stop anywhere, meaning that the single line tablets would have to be exchanged on the move at East Newport and at Wormit; however it did stop momentarily at East Newport. Nevertheless it then reached Wormit in four minutes from departure instead of the six minutes from passing allowed by the schedule. The WTT normally allowed eight minutes for service trains stopping at both West Newport and Wormit.

The Inspector's report has detailed evidence of unusual markings found on the rails, from just outside the tunnel and all the way through it. He believed that excess speed had caused the tender wheels, and probably those of the engine too, to lift off the rails. He also thought that the tender had tilted so far that it was scraping along the tunnel wall and that the buffing gear between it and the engine had become caught, preventing it righting itself when it emerged from the tunnel. The Report contains much detail about where the marks appeared on the rails in the tunnel together with speculation about how they had been caused.

The engine turned over on its left side and mounted the Down platform, damaging part of the canopy in the process. The first coach of train No.123 ended up across the Down line and Down platform on its side, while the second was derailed but remained upright against the Up platform. The third vehicle went off its bogies on its side on the Down platform while the fourth came to a stop leaning to the left with its front end on the platform and the rear on the rails at the tunnel mouth. The rest of the train remained on the rails but (terrifyingly for the occupants no doubt) still in the tunnel.

The Black Five and its tender were superficially damaged although it looked to be much worse at the time. They were drawn away from the scene on their wheels. The first coach was almost destroyed while the leading ends of the next three were badly damaged.

Evidence

Because of the injuries he had suffered it was not until 8 September that Driver Low could be interviewed and his evidence taken down. He had entered railway service in 1935 and had been a driver since 1947. On the fateful day he booked on at 11.45am and the outward run to Tayport had been uneventful. He readily admitted that he knew he was late in leaving Tayport but said that it was not his practice to try to make up lost time, nor had he intended to do so on this occasion.

The engine was inclined to prime and he had difficulty in opening the cylinder cocks. It primed as he applied the brakes approaching East Newport where the signalman had given the driver a caution signal, as required by the Rules. The train came to a stand while Driver Low tried with difficulty to open the cocks and eventually succeeded whereupon he restarted. The Inspector believed that Low had been unable to close the regulator after East Newport because the engine was still priming – he thus opened it fully once more but was uncertain whether he had succeeded in shutting it again. When questioned by Colonel McMullen Driver Low described the run to Wormit thus: *'Well everything was going quite normal Sir, and approaching the Wormit Distant as we turned the hill again, the water gave me trouble with my vacuum, and I was trying to keep the brake off as much as possible and regulate the speed of my train for entering the tunnel, and everything was going quite all right. I couldn't possibly get the cylinder cocks opened on this occasion and the regulator was not properly closed. That was the only trouble I had coming back and that was causing the catching of the water, but I am not very sure. But by the time I got to the tunnel everything was more or less in control and rounding the bend I can still remember the tender lifting and that is when the accident took place, derailment. We were swung round, battered about in the cab of course being off the road, and I must have pulled the brake off with me when I was thrown across the cab. There was a lurch. I got back and was able to apply the brake and pulled up just as the engine was about a coach length outside the tunnel.'*

The Inspector, questioning Driver Low further, recorded that he found it very difficult to elicit from the driver's answers exactly what information he wished to convey. Low was surprised to learn that the tender handbrake was found to be fully on and could not account for it. He admitted he knew he was breaking the Rules by carrying unauthorised passengers on the footplate but was emphatic that he was driving and that nobody else had touched the controls. The unauthorised passengers were on the fireman's side and he said he was not talking to them about the method of driving the engine. He would never allow anyone else to do the driving, not even the fireman.

Although he had signed for his route knowledge of the Tayport branch on 24 March 1955 he had only worked it a few times (the last occasion he had driven passenger trains on the branch had been 12 April) and he did not know of the speed restrictions which applied between East and West Newport. He had not driven a 5MT regularly but felt that the controls were not too dissimilar to those on other engine types he had driven.

Guard Mills knew the line well, having been Tayport born and bred, but he now lived in Balmerino; he confirmed the double drawing up before departure from Tayport but said that the engine crew seemed to mistake the signal for the second draw forward as that for the right away. He had had to jump into the rear van and apply the vacuum brake to stop the train.

He said that *'the driver for some reason or other stopped at East Newport when he should have carried on'*. He thought perhaps that the signalman had dropped the single line tablet so he looked out of the right-hand side window but could see nothing amiss. He therefore looked out of the left side window and saw a lady on the platform opening a carriage door. He asked a porter *'Why is he stopping?'* to which the porter replied *'It's all right. There's a lady wanting to go on but she's only going to West'*. The driver then just moved off on his own without any further instructions.

The guard thought the train was travelling at 45-50mph when it passed Woodhaven, just to the west of West Newport station. He felt that the driver was going too fast and made a slight brake application to try to draw his attention but to no avail. He made a heavier application and thought he had got speed down to about 25-30 mph when they reached the tunnel. Thinking that the driver had control he released the brake as the train entered the tunnel.

The signalman at East Newport confirmed that he had given the driver the usual warning with a green hand signal, which had been acknowledged by a blast on the whistle.

The porter at West Newport (J. Mannion) had said that when the train passed his station he had not seen it, being busy in the booking office, but from the sound he believed it was going much faster than the first excursion. He also said that some waiting passengers had commented on this and he was certain that the engine was under steam.

The signalman at Tay Bridge South (R. White) had a very good view of approaching trains over the top of the tunnel before they entered it. When he caught sight of train No.123 it was travelling faster than any other non-stopping train he had ever seen there – and he had worked in the box for twenty years. He was apprehensive about the token collection by hand and added *'I was waiting to see what speed it would come out of the tunnel. If at the same speed I was going to run out of the road for my own safety. I was not going to remain to receive the token at that speed'*. He was uncertain whether steam was on but *'it was blowing off steam and smoke from the funnel'*.

When he went out onto the platform Signalman White could hear that the train was making a noise 'like a pneumatic drill' and when the tender came out of the tunnel it started to fall over to the left side and ploughed into the platform. *'It went right up into the air with nothing visible except steam, smoke and fire coming from it. The first coach went straight up in the air, the second to the right and the third followed the first one'*.

Some children and a porter and a goods shunter were on the platform at Wormit and hearing the strange noises from the tunnel ran for their lives, the porter (R. Henderson) moving the children away into safety.

A number of the passengers gave evidence and those who were used to the line confirmed that the train had seemed to be travelling at an excessive speed. The Organiser, the Rev. John Innes of Morison Congregational Church, said that when the train went into the tunnel there was a screeching grating noise 'like a tramcar grinding round a sharp curve'. Some local residents also gave evidence and none thought that the brakes were being applied as the train passed their houses.

Events at Tayport

So what had gone wrong? To establish this we must look back, as did the Inspector, at what had happened while the Sunday School picnics were in progress. Once both trains had been stabled the crews joined the picnic party at the recreation ground, Tayport East Common, and during this time some of the excursionists went to visit the signalman in the South Box. At one stage Driver Low returned to his engine and made up the fire so that it would be ready for the return journey. At about 4.30pm Guard Mills and Low's fireman (Cowie) left the picnic and went to a shop for tea and then to a pub where they were later joined by Driver Low and Guard Thomson of train No.121.

About 5pm the driver and fireman of No.121 returned from the picnic to their train, knowing that they were due to leave Tayport as soon as possible after 6pm, instead of 6.30pm as had originally been booked. Guard Thomson later said that he did not know of the altered arrangements although he almost certainly had been told. Thus he did not leave the pub until 6.10pm, by which time the train had been detained some twenty minutes' waiting for him.

Driver Low left the pub about 5.30pm to draw his train onto the Down main line where it stood at the North Box Home signal; he then returned to the pub at 5.50pm and remained there with his guard and fireman until 6.25pm. Each said they had drunk two pints of beer although

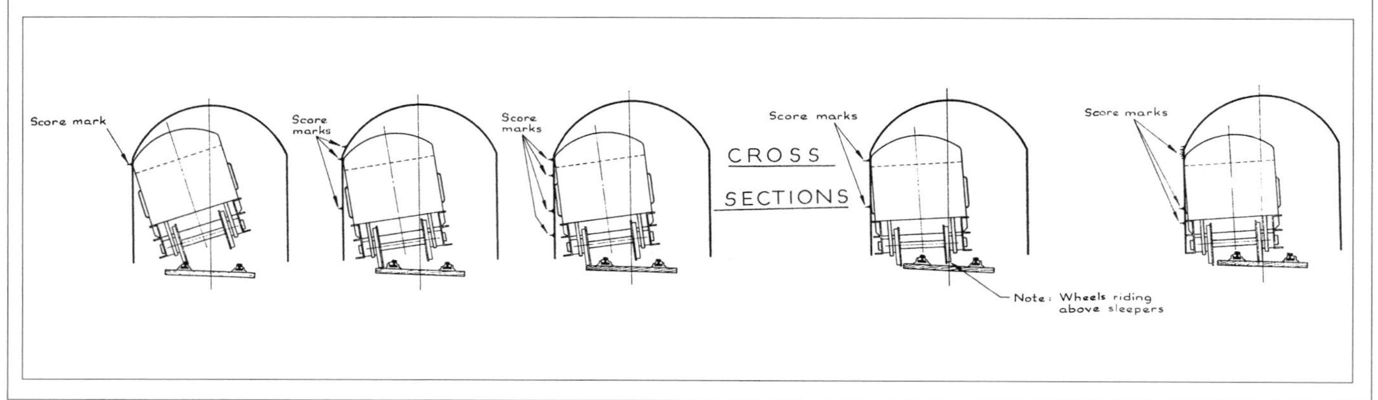

Top left. **The spectator's view. Work progresses on the day after the accident, Sunday 29 May 1955. Photograph G.C. Bett.**

Bottom left. **The site begins to clear. One passenger, Alan Fenton who was seven at the time, said, when interviewed in 1985, that he had good cause to recall the event. His father had seen sparks as the train went through the tunnel and when the train stopped his carriage was clear of it and he threw his son out of the window to safety – where he landed in a nettle bed ! Photograph J. Page.**

Driver Low said he did not finish the second.

After train No.122 had departed the signalman at Tayport North lowered his Home signal at 6.24pm but the crew of train No.123 did not return until 6.38pm. Before the double draw-up took place several adults and children climbed onto the footplate where the driver was explaining the controls to them. There were still 8-10 children on the footplate at the first draw forward.

Other Evidence

The Rev. Innes said that he and some children had been invited onto the footplate before departure from Tayport and that when the time for the draw-ups came the driver had said he'd take them 'the length of the platform'. He went very gently and slowly. Rev. Innes was asked whether the driver seemed 'normal': *'He did. He and the fireman had played football with our men most of the afternoon. When we broke for tea the fireman went for a look round. The driver was playing again after tea with some of the BB officers and senior boys.'*

Mr T.P. Williamson, the acting Inspector for the Tayport branch, told the inquiry that he had walked the line from Wormit towards Newport two days prior to the crash and saw no fresh marks on the tunnel brickwork. On the night of the crash he had again walked through the tunnel after 8.45pm and saw nothing, such as a broken rail, which could have caused the accident.

The relief Station Master at Tayport was John Legget and he told of the arrangements for handling the excursions on their arrival from Dundee. He had gone off duty at 5.40pm but returned at 6.40pm to see the train out. He said the draw forward signal was misinterpreted and the train made to set off – he told the guard to jump in and stop the train.

When interviewed, the Shed Master at Dundee Tay Bridge said he had received no previous reports of crews leaving engines unattended nor of drinking while on duty. Both were serious offences and he would discipline anyone who did either. Drivers had been reminded about not carrying any unauthorised passengers on the footplate in February, April and May of 1954.

Three residents of Wormit including John Dott, a student pharmacist who later took over the pharmacy in Tayport, had noticed how fast the train was going – much faster than was normal.

The engine was examined afterwards, both on site and at St Rollox Works, and the regulator valve was found to be closed, the reverser at 25%, the vacuum brake handle in mid-position and the tender handbrake on. Apart from damage sustained in the accident, everything was found to be in good condition with all equipment in working order. After repair at St Rollox 45458 was back in service by 18 August.

Test Runs

Three test runs were undertaken between Tayport and Wormit on Thursday 11 August using another Black 5, No.45384, hauling seven coaches and a dynamometer car. The first run was taken at the sort of speeds that the excursion should have been worked, without stopping at East Newport. This made for 26mph at the tunnel mouth, 22mph over the facing points and 16mph through the station.

The second run was as the train had actually been worked as far as the Tay Bridge South Distant signal, where the driver made a sharp brake application. Speed was then 33mph at the tunnel mouth, 18mph at the points and 10mph through the station.

On the final test it was intended to attain the maximum speed possible while still observing the restrictions through Wormit. This time speed rose to 48mph and after braking sharply in advance of the Distant signal the tunnel was entered at 15mph and the train was stopped in Wormit station.

Conclusion

The Inspector was satisfied that nothing was wrong with the track, the engine or the train but that the cause of the train's derailment was it being driven at very excessive speed over the sharp curve in the tunnel. He was certain that the speed of the excursion train 'could not have been less than 50mph and that it might have been nearer to 55mph'.

Priming was seen to be a contributory cause in that Driver Low was worried about the possibility of damage to a cylinder, which is why he allowed the train to stop at East Newport. Low knew he was partly responsible for the late start from Tayport and also that he had two unauthorised persons on the footplate. The driver had been drinking but not excessively.

The Inspector could not understand why the driver did not shut the regulator as soon as the train reached the down gradient in order to let it coast easily to Wormit as proved possible by test run No.1. The large ejector could have been used to blow water out of the vacuum pipes before the train had gathered much speed but it seems that Driver Low was using it with the regulator open. Apparently he did not attempt to close it until after the train had passed West Newport and then experienced difficulty in so doing because of the priming. By that time the train was approaching the Distant signal at between 45 and 50mph, considerably in excess of the maximum permitted 25mph.

'In spite of Low's firm statement to the contrary' the Report records, *'there can be no doubt at all that he did not apply the brakes until the engine was about to enter or was just inside the tunnel, and it is by no means certain whether even then they were applied by him or by the guard. By that time the speed had risen to 50-55 mph and the overturning movement started as the train entered the sharp curve, before the application had time to take effect'.*

Colonel McMullen indicated that on the second test run he had felt a slight sway on the engine where the curve reversed but he did not think it could have been nearly so severe as the type of lurch that Driver Low had said he had experienced on previous trips. It seemed possible therefore that, on the few occasions on which he had driven a passenger train over the section in question, he had been in the habit of entering the tunnel at speeds as high as 40 to 45 mph, way in excess of the limit.

The Inspector felt that the excursion train had not been under full control and, had it not been derailed, would still have been travelling at some 40-45 mph when it emerged from the tunnel. *'This can, therefore, be no case of misjudgement and I can attribute it to nothing less than sheer recklessness. It seems possible that Low may have been 'showing off' to his unauthorised passengers'.*

The Colonel continued: *'I cannot disassociate the recklessness of Driver Low in the running of this train from his highly irresponsible behaviour while on duty at Tayport. Strictly contrary to the Rules, he went drinking in a public house about quarter of a mile away, and he went there a second time; as a result the train started late from Tayport. He allowed his engine to be unattended for some time on a running line, which is also against the Rules; consequently the boiler became so full of water that it primed badly. In addition, he allowed unauthorised passengers to travel on the footplate; again, this is strictly forbidden by an Instruction about which he had been repeatedly reminded. I am unable to say whether Low's judgement had been affected by the drink he had taken but on a hot day even a small amount of alcohol may have been sufficient to slow down his reactions and possibly also to make him a little reckless.*

'Low is 39 years of age and he assured me he had no worries either in his work or at home. He has been a driver for seven years and had a good record. It is to his credit that he did not attempt to excuse himself for his irregular conduct at Tayport'.

Both guards were criticised for going for a drink at Tayport, thereby causing the late departures of their trains. Colonel McMullen also discussed Guard Mills' actions in respect to the brake; he considered that Mills *'erred in his judgement in not making the full application earlier but I am not inclined to criticise him unduly. A guard will always expect the driver to exercise the necessary control of the speed to comply with*

Cleaning some of the last of the debris (the shattered coach body was simply lifted out of the way to be dealt with in due course) on Monday 30 May 1955. Photograph courtesy Dundee Courier.

A distant view. Photograph G.C. Bett.

restrictions, and will naturally be reluctant to act on his own initiative, essential though this may be on some occasions'.

Colonel McMullen felt there were similarities to the accident at Sutton Coldfield on 23 January 1955 where the Inspector had concluded that the driver had forgotten about a speed restriction. His report concluded with the following remarks:

'It is disturbing to find that when certain responsible members of the staff had of necessity to spend some time at an outstation with little active work to do, they did not have the self discipline to keep themselves interested without breaking the Rules.

'There is little more to be said in this case except to repeat the statement in the Report on the Sutton Coldfield accident that derailments due to excessive speed on plain track have been very rare. Such derailments caused by the recklessness of a driver are still more unusual.

'I have mentioned that there was no speed restriction on the sharp curve in the tunnel on account of the permanent restriction over the points a short distance ahead, and there was no speed restriction sign for the latter. Such signs were in use on the former London and North Eastern Railway of which this branch line was a part, but it was not the practice to install them in such circumstances. A speed restriction has been imposed on the curve since the accident and a sign has been erected and, while I do not think that these precautions should be necessary in such a place, I consider that the action taken is sound'.

The Driver on Trial

Unusually, the incident led to a prosecution. Driver Low was charged with culpable homicide, appearing at a preliminary hearing at Cupar Sheriff Court. He then came before Lord Mackintosh at the High Court in Perth, on February 8th 1956 where he pled not guilty to the allegation of driving in a culpable and reckless manner and at an excessive speed.

Evidence was given by many people, fifty-seven of whom were witnesses for the Crown. Among the passengers was the Rev. Innes – he estimated the speed at between 50 and 60 mph and said the train 'was going like the Flying Scotsman compared with the speed of the train on the previous year's outing to Tayport'.

Alexander Low gave his evidence on the third day of the trial and spoke for well over an hour. He declared himself astonished at allegations of excessive speed and considered it 'out of the question' that he had entered the tunnel at 50mph and at half a mile from it his maximum speed was 40mph. He was in no hurry to get back to Dundee and was not trying to make up time. He was unable to give an explanation for the derailment but it was certainly not because the train was going too fast.

After arrival at Tayport he had joined the picnickers and played with the children and had a game of football with the older people. The Rev. Innes confirmed this. On returning to the station a number of boys and young men came to the engine and he showed them round it. Although it was against the rules, he gave them a short demonstration run up the platform – for their own safety he had kept them on the footplate. When the Defence Advocate, Douglas Johnstone QC, questioned him further he said he had difficulty getting them all off the engine and one boy and a young man simply stayed on board. He then received a signal which he interpreted as a 'right away' but now understood it to have meant 'stop short'.

At no time during the journey from Tayport did the extra persons on the footplate get in the way of the crew and nor did they interfere with the handling of the engine. Driver Low claimed he had lost control when the tender lurched in the middle of the tunnel. He had stopped at East Newport because 'the fore end of the

Aftermath – the Black Five 45458 waits in the yard at Wormit with customary tarpaulin for the onward journey to St Rollox. Both photographs G.C. Bett.

engine was full of water' i.e. priming was occurring. He had difficulty all the way after that and when he entered the tunnel he abandoned trying to open the cylinder drain cocks in order to apply the brakes. When the tender lurched he was thrown across the cab and he pulled the brake off again in the process. He had subsequently managed to re-apply it with his left hand – his right arm was broken by then.

When the tender went over on its side a pipe burst and he could see nothing for steam. The brake type was unfamiliar – that on LNER locos went up and down whereas on the Black 5 it went across.

Guard Mills did not see or feel anything to suggest that Low had applied the brakes before entering the tunnel and agreed that if both driver and guard applied the vacuum brake at the same time neither would know that the other had done so. After the crash he had helped to get the driver out.

Another driver and Trade Union official, William Paterson, considered a Black 5 unsuitable for the Tayport line because of the severe curvature and another driver indicated that they were only used when no tank engines were available. He said that the track condition inside the tunnel had improved since the crash – there had always been oscillation of the tender when such engines were used.

The Wormit Station Master, Benjamin Henderson, had gone immediately to the Tay Bridge South signalbox to check the signalling apparatus. When questioned he said that the train should be doing no more than 10mph for token exchanges.

The Crown's case, the Defence declared in the summing up to the jury, was that having driven carefully for the whole day up until about West Newport Alexander Low suddenly went berserk or mad and rushed the whole of his train into Wormit tunnel – that he hurled the train into the tunnel wall regardless of the consequences. Can you believe that? the jury was asked.

If there was any excessive speed going through the tunnel then it did not arise out of any criminal indifference to the consequences but it may possibly have arisen as a result of an error of judgement on the driver's part. The jury *'could not convict a man of culpable homicide on an error of judgement or even on carelessness or proof of negligence. It must be gross or culpable negligence'.*

The Defence Advocate also said that it was significant that there had since been a radical alteration in the speed permitted from unlimited or 45 mph when running tender first down to 30mph over the whole line and down to 15mph, with the erection of a caution sign, outside the tunnel.

Before the jury retired Lord Mackintosh told them to consider – was there wicked and criminal recklessness? Was the train travelling at 50mph plus in the tunnel as the railway experts had said? If that was so and unless there was some reasonable explanation the inference was gross and indeed recklessness in his driving. On the other hand if they thought there may have been other reasons for the crash than speed and they thought this had not been sufficiently excluded and they had reasonable doubt, it was their duty to bring in a verdict of not proven or not guilty. The presence of unauthorised passengers on the footplate was no concern of the Court – this was a matter for disciplinary action by BR.

The jury of nine men and three women retired for only thirty minutes on 10 February 1956 and Alexander Low was acquitted by majority verdict.

Strange Footnote

The through trains from Tayport to Leuchars Junction ceased less than a year after the crash when the line southwards from Tayport was closed to all traffic, from 3 January 1956. The branch then had only a suburban service. *The Courier* reported on 29 May 1961 that May 28th was a fated day for Wormit, for it was exactly six years to the day of the 1955 incident that another train was derailed in the station. This was the six-car 1.25pm DMU from Tayport to Dundee which was carrying about 60 passengers, including some Girl Guides going to their annual church parade in Dundee. When it emerged from the tunnel at Wormit, the leading coach was 'caught by points and ran onto the Up track'. The trailing bogie left the rails and slightly damaged the track. No one was injured and the whole train remained upright.

According to the newspaper the passengers descended from the train in the tunnel although, as with the earlier incidents, it must have been difficult to open the doors sufficiently wide. A special train was sent from Dundee an hour later to collect them so that they could complete their journey.

The derailed bogie was back on the track by 3.45pm and the train was then driven back into the tunnel, presumably to reach the correct line. There is no mention of whether it was then driven across the bridge on its wheels or whether the bogie was put onto a wheel skate – if not then there must have been some apprehension on the part of the crew about crossing that wide expanse with a possibly dodgy bogie beneath them...

A peculiar footnote – a Metro-Cammell DMU straddles the track six years to the day after train No.123's destruction. Photograph courtesy Dundee *Courier*.

Endpiece

Farewell to summer. As yet without a name, 21C163 (later 34063 229 SQUADRON) coasts through the countryside 'somewhere in England' during 1948. (Actually the site is Polhill, near the tunnel of that name, between Dunton Green and Knockholt.) Photograph The Transport Treasury.